Home.

Home is inspired by all of the wonderful clients I have met and worked with over the years. I truly believe that the home is an extension of who we are and what we represent. This book explains how anyone can achieve a beautifully decorated and meaningful place to call home.

Home.

The Elements of Decorating

EMMA BLOMFIELD

hardie grant books

Contents

4   Dining rooms

5   Bedrooms

1

Decorating basics

Decorating
your home

Decorating your home is investing in your family's pleasure and happiness. However, knowing exactly how to decorate a space is not an innate skill and some people need more help in this department than others. With a little guidance and direction, it's entirely possible for you to create a look you love and a home you are proud to show off. Of course, a beautiful home isn't all about what your guests think of the space. It's absolutely crucial that you and your family are in love with the space you've created and can happily call it 'home'.

This is your guidebook to carry with you throughout the decorating process, and it's a book you can continue to refer to over many years. The watercolour illustrations are eternally relevant and lend themselves to interpretation—rather than focusing on recreating all the elements within a photographic image, the illustrations will hopefully inspire your sense of fun and creativity. Not only are the illustrations timeless, the decorating methods are tried and tested; therefore the same rules will apply in decades to come. The book will guide you through the various ways you can achieve a stylish look, incorporating well-loved pieces as well as budget-friendly updates, without having to start from the ground up. It will show you that you don't have to spend tens of thousands of dollars to achieve a stylish and attractive home.

When entering a beautifully decorated space, people often won't be able to pinpoint what they like most because a stylish space will have various nooks and crannies to explore and discover. The goal isn't to have one item screaming for attention, it's about the journey through the room and discovering the bits and pieces on display. It's the ultimate compliment when guests enter your home and tell you how wonderful they think the space looks.

If you're wondering whether or not your home could do with a spruce up, think about how you feel about it. You may have lusted after a friend's beautiful home or wish something was different about your own place. Perhaps you can sense that something is missing from a room but you can't quite put your finger on it. Or maybe the rooms in your house don't meet your family's needs and wants.

The quickest way to identify whether a room could do with some amendments is to take a photo of it. You'll instantly be drawn to any areas that need help—those areas are much more obvious in two-dimensional form than they are in real life. You may notice gaps between grouped items or that the positioning of certain pieces is slightly off. These things don't always stand out as you walk around a room, so capturing them in a photo will show you exactly where you need to pay more attention.

If you aren't able to pinpoint issues by photographing the room, try pretending that your home is up for sale and you are preparing for an inspection by prospective buyers. Look beyond your furniture and don't let it crowd your view. You need to look at the bare bones, such as the walls, floors and traffic flow, rather than the colour, texture and patterns showing up in the pieces already in the rooms. Chances are, you'll want to replace a number of elements, and taking a step back and detaching yourself from these pieces will make the process easier.

DECORATOR'S TIP

Decorating relates to the room as a whole—the overall, cohesive look of the space— including the furnishings, floor coverings, fabrics, paint colours and window dressings.

Styling relates to the smaller elements in the room. It involves arranging items such as trays, candles, trinkets and jewellery boxes in a pleasing way. See chapter 9 (page 147) for more on styling.

Decorating basics

HOME

It's important that you are committed to the decorating process from the start, instead of waiting until you can afford really nice things. You will probably never be truly financially ready, so make the most of what you already have. Often an objective view is all it takes to change your opinion on the pieces you already own.

This book will teach you that decorating for practicality is possible. The magazine cut-out you aspire to isn't necessarily practical or useful for the way you live—but that doesn't mean you can't use it for inspiration.

Being realistic throughout the decorating process will pay off in the long run and will stop you from making expensive mistakes. Making practical purchases is all about buying items you like and will love for years to come. You don't want to invest your hard-earned money in a big-ticket item like a sofa simply because it's trendy. Trendy additions are only a good idea if you buy them knowing that in a few months (or a few years at a stretch), you will still love them. It's better to experiment with trends by choosing smaller, more mobile pieces that you are happy to replace in the near future.

The five elements
of decorating

Pulling a room together is a lengthy process. It's not something you can achieve in an afternoon and unfortunately no magic wands exist yet. The good news is that you don't need to be swimming in cash to have a stylish-looking home. Familiarising yourself with the following five elements of decorating will help you visualise your finished space and fit out your home like a professional, while keeping within your budget. Ultimately you will feel happy each time you walk into your home.

1. NEEDS + WANTS

When starting your room makeover or decorating process from scratch, it's crucial to consider and identify the needs of the space as well as the people who use it. There's no use decorating a room if you aren't going to take practicality and usefulness into consideration. Ask yourself and the rest of your family the following questions:

- Who uses the room?
- What do you use the room for and how do you use it?
- Do you use the room for different activities throughout the day and evening?

Your decorating choices will impact heavily on everyone who uses the room, so it's important to consider every potential use when planning the decoration. When you consult the other members of your household, you may find you have overlooked a significant need of someone who shares the space.

2. COLOUR + PATTERN

It's wise to select three to five colours for your room's colour palette. These don't have to be colours on opposite sides of the colour wheel. You can easily make up the three to five colours with sandy taupes, whites or even blacks, with pops of pink, aqua or yellow. In fact, it's often best to use relatively neutral tones for two or three of the five colours so that you then have two or three stand-out colours to use as accents when choosing your soft furnishings. If you are working with an existing space, look to your art or rug to inspire your colour palette. You can then repeat these three to five colours in items around the room, such as bookshelf ornaments, a coffee-table tray or sofa cushions. See page 36 for more information on selecting your colour palette.

Adding pattern to a room creates interest as well as giving your room depth and character. Use pattern in your soft furnishings, curtains or smaller elements such as candle jars or vases, working existing colours into the pattern to get the mix right. If you don't feel confident with picking patterns and mixing them up, the trick is to select matching tones within the pattern options and work in solid colours. For example, if your rug features navy and peach tones, select patterned objects in light blues, corals and tangerines to keep the base tones similar. This will result in a more pleasing overall look.

Decorating basics

HOME

3. SHAPE + SIZE

Varying the shapes and sizes you use is the key to creating a cohesive and harmonious space. Contrast the flat items in the room, such as books, shelves and tables, with a taller object like a cylindrical vase or a table lamp. Objects with visual weight provide balance and scale to the overall look—something that paint and flooring can't do.

4. PLACEMENT

Achieving visual balance can be tricky, but all it takes is the right placement of furniture and decor. Odd numbers work best when grouping items together. Repetition of pattern or colour gives the eyes a place to rest, meaning they aren't darting here, there and everywhere when you enter a space—rather, you are drawing the eyes to a pleasing spot. Eye strain is not the aim of the game when decorating!

5. LIGHTING

Lighting is one of the most important elements in decorating, yet it is often overlooked. It is commonly put on the end of the 'to do' list when renovating or building a home. Perhaps there are so many other elements screaming for attention, or the budget is wearing thin. However, a little thought and planning when it comes to lighting will take you a long way towards a beautiful space.

A well-lit space has a positive effect on our mood. Think about how natural light affects us, making us feel happy and bright. Artificial light also affects our demeanour, so lighting choices are an important element in the decorating game.

Lighting also has a powerful effect on the atmosphere of a room. If you enter a room that is blaring with bright and clinical white light, you'll feel uncomfortable and uneasy. However, if you enter a room that features a table lamp or two as well as some dimly lit overhead lighting, you'll feel more relaxed and at ease.

Types of lighting to consider include downlights (always installed with dimmer switches so that you can control the level of light required at different times of the day), lamps, pendants, wall sconces and candles.

DECORATOR'S TIP

Be sure to select warm white globes over cool white ones. Warm light creates a much more harmonious and relaxing atmosphere, not to mention it being much kinder to your skin tone.

Decorating basics

HOME

Finding inspiration

After deciding you are going to take the plunge and redecorate, collecting inspiration can be a daunting task. However, once you start looking for inspiration, you'll realise that it's actually all around you. Sometimes you just need to take a slightly more objective view.

WHERE TO LOOK FOR INSPIRATION

Start by taking inspiration from the landscape around your home. Do you have a tropical oasis in your backyard or do you back onto a national park? Is your home by the seaside or in the midst of an urban jungle?

Be considerate towards the architecture of your home—an old Victorian terrace house will need very different treatment to a weatherboard cottage by the beach.

Have your travels inspired a whole new look for your home? Bring out your treasured photos and list elements of buildings that you've seen overseas or interstate that you could incorporate into your home. Don't forget to jump online, too. A whole world of inspiration is just a click away, from blogs to lifestyle websites brimming with decor ideas and creative brilliance (see page 180).

Perhaps a favourite movie has inspired your redecorating project. Hollywood movies such as *The Family Stone*, *Father of the Bride* and *Something's Gotta Give* all feature beautiful family homes brimming with ideas to borrow. They may not be on the same budget scale as you, but can still be a great place to source inspirational elements.

Old-school coffee table books and magazines are also a brilliant pool of decorating inspiration. They provide a tangible source of inspiration that you can throw in your bag as you hit the shops, or leave pinned above your desk as a visual reminder of where your project is headed.

Identifying
your style

Analyse your existing decor—does it reflect your own style, personality and taste, as well as that of the other members of your family or household? Have you inherited furniture here and there or did you move in with your partner and make do until you could afford to upgrade? Now is the time to start doing your research.

If you are finding it difficult to identify your style, don't be too concerned. It is often easier to identify styles we don't like rather than immediately pinpointing those we do. If you feel you fall into this category, start by flicking through some of your favourite home decor magazines or books, or searching through blogs and other inspirational websites. Have a pen and paper with you to jot down anything you notice.

To really home in on your style, list common elements you see appearing in the images and ideas you've been collecting or admiring from magazines, books, Pinterest mood boards, your friends' homes, visual merchandising from retail stores or just everyday life. These common elements could be as simple as observing that you keep selecting sofas in charcoal grey fabrics with buttoned back cushions or that every living room you like features a sisal rug and cushions in navy and white stripes, indicating a Hamptons look (see page 22).

Another excellent way to solve your style mystery is to ask friends and family if they can help you narrow it down. Chances are they've spent numerous hours in your home observing the pieces you have on display and they could very well have bought you gifts for your home, too. Getting an outsider's perspective can open your eyes to how your style has evolved since you moved into your home.

Remember, you are never too old (or too young) to identify and develop your style. Your style will always be evolving and changing, so what you were drawn to when you first moved out of home will almost certainly have changed by the time you start a family and then again by the time your children grow up and move out.

TAKE NOTES

Taking note of some of the following small and seemingly insignificant details is the quickest way to identify your style.

Colours: Are there any combinations you have been drawn to? Are there colours you'd really like to avoid having in your home? Do the pieces of art you are drawn to often feature the same colours and patterns?

Shapes: Are lots of linear items appearing in your notes or are you drawn to rounded objects, such as oval dining tables or circular coffee tables?

Metals: Do you prefer the cool, slick, stainless steel look to a burnished antique gold? Metals will instantly give away your style—stainless or brushed steel screams modern and contemporary, whereas brass and antique silver give off more traditional, classic vibes.

Furniture styles: Have you been noting down that you prefer rolled, rounded sofa arms to thin, slim-line arms? Do all the dining tables you like have turned timber legs as opposed to steel legs and glass tops?

Features of popular interior styles

The next few pages show examples of furniture styles, decorative elements and textures that you can take note of when deciphering your interior style.

HAMPTONS

- Linen sofas
- Navy and white colour combinations
- Stripes
- Sisal rugs
- Nautical elements

SCANDINAVIAN

- Oak timber
- Monochrome colour combinations
- Sheepskin rugs
- White walls
- Light timber floorboards

FRENCH PROVINCIAL

- Turned-timber elements
- Iron baskets
- Toile patterns
- Clay-pot ornaments
- Floral patterns
- Brass trimmings
- Muted colours
- Roman numerals

ECLECTIC

- A mix-and-match look
- Pattern clashes
- Unique
- Layers
- Ikat patterns
- Earth-toned colour combinations
- A warm and 'lived-in' look

MODERN MINIMALIST

- Sleek lines
- Glass accents
- Stainless-steel finishes
- Flat, linear surfaces
- Leather sofas
- A statement swivel armchair

INDUSTRIAL

- Iron
- Raw timber
- Numbers
- Concrete
- Primary-colour combinations
- Exposed bricks and beams

Decorating basics

HOME

ORIENTAL

- Bold, dominant colours
- Red, jade and aqua colour combinations
- High-gloss, lacquered timber
- Intricately carved furniture
- Bamboo elements
- Handpainted furniture

MOROCCAN

- Intricate patterns
- Mosaics
- Wedding blankets
- Kilim rugs
- Leather poufs
- Brightly coloured ceramics

RETRO

- 1950s inspired
- Mid-tone timber
- Walnut timber
- Framed vintage posters
- Moulded ply and fibreglass furniture
- Orange, green, yellow and red colour combinations

Decorating basics

HOME

TRIBAL

- Beading
- Feathers
- Dark-chocolate timber
- Carved-timber furniture
- Tribal juju hats as art
- Kilim rugs

COUNTRY/RUSTIC

- Raw, unpolished timber
- Checked patterns
- Gingham fabrics
- Antlers
- Ticking stripes
- Hessian
- Weathered or patina-finished timbers
- Knitted blankets

TRADITIONAL

- Classic and elegant furniture
- Deep-cushioned sofas
- Curved angles
- Tufting
- Fringing
- Plump scatter cushions

Decorating basics

HOME

Combining interior styles

Perhaps you find it difficult to identify with just one interior style. Styles combine well when they are complementary, so you can create a harmonious look by merging elements.

How do you put different styles together seamlessly? Identify any common elements from the styles and think about any conflicts. Your existing furniture will guide you here—do a bit of research into your own home. Look at the textures already in the room as well as the colour scheme, and note any elements that match the styles listed on pages 22–25. If you can identify any common links then you'll be able to see where your styles overlap. Refer back to the style lists to see what other elements you could add to your rooms to create a cohesive look. You'll also need to consider the architecture of the room. For example, will the timbers clash or complement?

STYLES THAT BLEND SEAMLESSLY

- Hamptons + Traditional
- Country/rustic + Industrial
- Oriental + Eclectic
- Moroccan + Eclectic
- Scandinavian + Modern minimalist

These style pairings work well because they contain common elements. For example, the furniture pieces appearing in most Hamptons themes are relatively classic pieces with rolled arms and linen fabrics, which echo Traditional style beautifully. Country/rustic style blends effortlessly with Industrial style because both styles feature raw textural elements, such as exposed brick, rustic timbers and beaten-up metals. Oriental and Eclectic

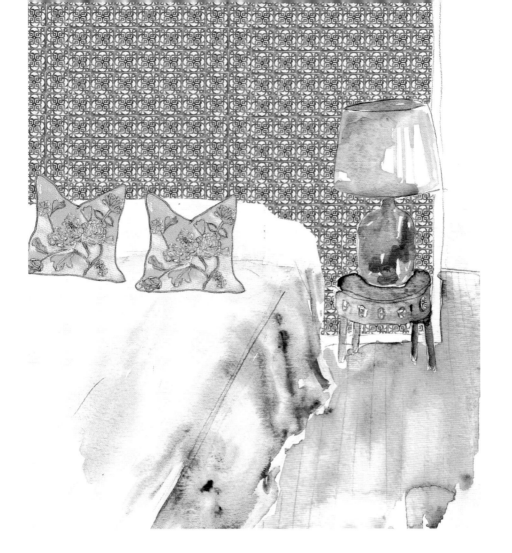

styles both feature strong, bold colours such as indigo, teal, red and yellow, and the patterns associated with both styles are quite busy so when they are paired up the common elements work well together. Moroccan style is known for its mishmash approach so combining this with Eclectic style produces a beautiful array of colour, pattern and texture. Scandinavian style is relatively minimalist so pairing it with the sleek lines and stainless steel finishes of Modern minimalist ensures a solid style.

Assessing
your space

Once you have clearly identified your style and taste, it's time to analyse and assess the space in which you live. Living in a space for a long period of time can mean you start to overlook problem areas that guests would notice instantly. Perhaps there are places where paint is peeling, some tatty scatter cushions, well-worn rugs or mismatched armchairs you've been making do with since you moved in five years ago.

It's time to start making notes and stop ignoring all those little problems that can add up over time and cause you to fall out of love with your home. Start by making a list of your aspirations, hopes and dreams. You can go for an overall feel for your entire home or you can focus on one room at a time. I find it's best to focus on one room at a time, as it means you'll put all your energy into completing one space before moving on to the next. It also allows clearer focus and stops you from becoming overwhelmed with a much bigger project. But remember, it is also important to have the big picture in mind to ensure some consistency between your rooms.

QUESTIONS TO CONSIDER

- How do I want to feel when I enter the room?
- How do I want my family to interact here?
- What do I want my guests to feel when they come to visit?
- What do I definitely not want to feel when I come home?

The answers to these questions may surprise you. Don't forget to consult the other people who use the room, as they may raise some important questions for you, too.

To get yourself and your home ready for redecorating, it's vital to analyse the existing pieces in a room as well as the overall space. You can do this by asking more specific questions about the elements in the room. The following questions will help you work out what is and what isn't working in the current space.

Layout

Is the room too cramped? Does the room have too much empty, blank space? Is the room an awkward shape? Are there lots of entry points to consider? Are there too many obstacles blocking the walkways? Is the TV blocked from view? Are there too many focal points in the room? Are there any unused items in the room, such as the TV, second sofa or coffee table? Is the furniture placement blocking the natural flow of traffic?

Lighting

Is the room currently too dark or too light? Is there enough natural light? What are the options for task lighting, e.g. lamps for reading or working? Do I need curtains and/or blinds for light filtering or privacy (or both)? Would installing some dimmer switches benefit the space?

Decorating basics

HOME

Furniture and fixtures

Is there enough seating space? Is there too much seating space? Are the floors hard and cold in winter? Are there enough surfaces to hold everyday household items? Do I need more colour in the room? Is there adequate storage? Are the textures in the room working together?

WHAT NEXT?

After carefully analysing the features within the room, you need to make a list of any particular items you want to work with—perhaps a lamp your mother gave you or an ottoman you inherited. What can be sold, given away or thrown away? It may even be helpful to walk through the room with coloured sticky notes identifying 'keep', 'chuck' and 'sell' items as you go.

Think about whether any items that make it to the 'keep' list need some additional love, such as a coat of paint, re-upholstering or a good steam clean.

PROJECT 'TO DO' LIST

By now your lists may be growing long. If you have a large home or a lot of possessions this could be where you come unstuck and either give up or jump ahead and start the purchasing process. It's important not to become disillusioned at this stage. Careful planning will result in fewer mistakes and frustrations. It would be wise to consolidate your lists into one overall project 'to do' list, showing projects in order of importance to help keep you on track.

DECORATOR'S TIP

Keep referring to your project 'to do' list, as well as your floor plan and mood board (see pages 32 and 34) to keep you on track, and ensure you only progress through the stages when your budget allows. It's easy to get caught up in the project and want to furnish the whole space in a weekend, but that's where you'll end up making expensive mistakes, regretting your choices and not falling in love with the final look. You could also end up with a 'catalogue look'—a tell-tale sign that you spent your weekend at a furniture superstore and made do with what you could find because you didn't have the patience to wait for it to come together naturally. Careful research will ensure you end up with a style and look that you truly love. It will also reflect the personalities of you and your family rather than your local furniture store's front window.

Decorating basics

HOME

Using a floor plan

Before you buy any furniture, it's sensible to measure your room and plan the best furniture layout options. This will allow you to create a number of different seating, sleeping or traffic-flow options that will help you determine what is most suitable for the space.

Often people make the mistake of buying the largest sofa that could possibly fit in the room. But the largest sofa won't necessarily fit with the room's proportions, nor will it help to create a cosy, conversational feel.

A floor plan also means less heavy lifting and furniture shuffling. Once you're happy with the layout, use masking tape to indicate where the big-ticket items (sofas, beds, dining tables or even rugs) will go. This will allow you to visualise the space more clearly, as well as making sure the furniture is placed where you want it when it is delivered.

When planning your furniture placement, don't forget to consider breathing room and traffic flow.

Breathing room: *A well-planned room will actually make good use of the available floor space without having all the furniture pushed up against the walls. A 20–30 cm (8–12 in) gap from the walls is ideal and, as unlikely as it seems, will actually make the room feel larger.*

Traffic flow: *Natural traffic flow will be determined by a number of factors, such as the position of doorways, where TV and power points have been installed, and the placement of the fireplace and large fixed furniture pieces, such as built-in bench seats or cupboards.*

Decorating basics

HOME

Using a
mood board

A mood board helps you to stay focused when decorating; it's a visual reference point for you to consult when you're shopping for furniture, picking paint colours or showing your builder or decorator your vision for the project.

There are no limitations when it comes to making your mood board—pin what you like and keep editing what you've pinned. Don't get caught up with budgets and trends just yet; that comes further down the track. For now just focus on where you see the project heading and your visual inspiration. Working out pricing and compromising on certain elements will come into play after this, but for now it's all about collating and editing images.

DIGITAL VERSUS TANGIBLE

Choose whichever medium you prefer to display your inspirational mood board. If you're opting for a physical mood board, an afternoon with some magazines, a pair of scissors and a corkboard and pins is all you need. Otherwise there are numerous websites you can use to create a virtual mood board, such as Pinterest or Houzz. There are even some apps listed in the Resource book (see page 183) that can help you create beautiful digital mood boards.

- Fabric swatches
- Wallpaper and paint samples
- Colour inspiration
- Runway fashion
- Ribbon/trims
- Catalogue cut-outs
- Magazine cut-outs
- Travel mementos

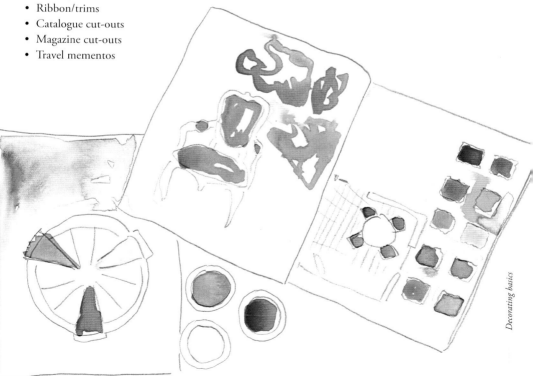

Decorating basics

HOME

Selecting your colour palette

Now is the time to consider colour choices for your room. As mentioned in 'Colour + pattern' (page 15), it's best to select three to five colours for a room.

Sometimes it's easier to start looking for furniture and decor to see what you like and allowing your colour palette to form from there, rather than going in with a strict colour palette to follow and failing to find anything that suits your vision.

We tend to choose big-ticket items like sofas, armchairs, dining chairs and dining tables in relatively neutral colours. This means your colour palette isn't restricted too early in the process. Once you've locked in some choices for these big-ticket items, you can experiment with colour palettes when choosing art, rugs, cushions and other soft furnishings.

The base colour of the neutral fabrics will help you determine whether your colour palette needs cool or warm tones. If you've chosen a charcoal grey sofa, your colour palette will be suited more to cool tones. If your sofa is beige or taupe, your colour palette will lean towards warmer tones. Play around with different options—you probably won't get it right the first time. You may need to gather fabric swatches or visit stores a number of times before you start to feel like your colour palette is forming.

- Navy + white + sandy beige
- Pink + orange + lime green
- Burgundy + navy + tan
- Mint green + peach + duck-egg blue
- Mauve + grey + charcoal
- Cobalt + sage green + soft grey
- Blueberry + raspberry + mint green
- Soft grey + charcoal + mustard
- Ochre + mustard + taupe
- Teal + purple + aqua

Decorating basics

HOME

Executing the look

The planning process in a decorating project is definitely time consuming, but it's worth putting in the extra effort so that you have a detailed plan to work from when it comes time to execute the look. While it's easy to get excited and jump ahead, following the steps on the previous pages will result in a much smoother execution.

Having a plan to follow means you don't have to contemplate as many decisions at once. You can refer back to your floor plan, mood board or colour palette to jog your memory while you're out shopping or as a guide when deciding on finishing touches.

So, once you're satisfied with your floor plan, mood board and colour palette it's time to dive into the fun part—spending your hard-earned cash on some great new pieces.

THE PURCHASING PROCESS

There are three important stages in the purchasing process: the big-ticket items, the soft furnishings and the finishing touches. Of all the areas where the decorating process can break down, the two most common are at the beginning of the purchasing process, when the first decisions are being made about which direction to take the decor in, and when it's time to put the finishing touches together.

1. Big-ticket items

When you are starting the decorating process from scratch, you will ideally buy your big-ticket items first (for example, a sofa, bed or table). The big-ticket items will be most prominent in the room. Opting for more neutral fabrics and materials when choosing these larger items will ensure longevity and practicality.

A neutral base also allows you to try many different looks in the space over the furniture's lifetime, as you can swap out soft furnishings with ease for a whole new look.

As you pick out your big-ticket items, add them to your mood board and keep checking that you are on the right path. Don't make any purchases until you are certain of your choices. You will find that your first choices for most items won't remain the same. It's okay to try several variations of one look until it feels right.

2. Soft furnishings

Once your mood board is up to date with your furniture choices, you can add in stage-two items, which include things such as rugs, artworks, cushions, curtains and lamps. These will tie the big-ticket items together. Continue to refer to your original vision for colour and texture inspiration—it will help make deciding on soft furnishings much easier. Remember the rule of three to five colours as you go. This will help keep you focused and you'll be able to identify potential items much faster.

Decorating basics

HOME

Select your rug first—it's much easier to match cushions and artwork to a rug than vice versa if you want a splash of colour on your floor. There are endless options for wall art, from digital canvases with blocks of geometric colour, to rustic metal sculptural pieces and framed family photos, but your choices for floor coverings are narrower. After selecting your rug (see 'Rugs 101' on page 166 for more information), bring out colours from the rug in your artwork, cushions and other elements. A nice touch would be to select a lampshade in similar hues or consider a neutral lampshade with a nice trim that works in with the rug.

3. Finishing touches

Stage three is often the stage where the decorating process is abandoned because the majority of the furniture is in place and you've lost your decorating willpower. Perhaps your bank account took a serious beating in stages one and two and you need some time to recover financially. The fun isn't over, though. The finishing touches are what make a room feel cosy and inviting, and without them you'll forever feel like something is lacking.

Finishing touches include:

- trinkets from your travels
- trays for coffee table items
- framed photos
- a vase of flowers
- a centrepiece for the dining table
- anything that will add personality, soul and character.

If you're starting to burn out creatively, it might be wise to take a break and live in the space a little longer before making any further decisions on your finishing touches. Time-out will give you perspective and perhaps even a different viewpoint.

Decorator's toolkit

Items you'll need to get you through the
decorating process include:

- pens, pencils and eraser
- notepad/scrapbook
- camera
- tape measure
- ruler
- scissors
- masking tape
- blu-Tack
- sticky notes
- hammer and nails
- hooks
- screws.

2

Entryways

Entryway decorating

Not all areas of your home are on show for your guests but your entryway will be seen by anyone entering or exiting your home. It should be an inviting area, and making it welcoming and pleasant is a nice way to give guests a taste of what's to come throughout the rest of the house.

The front entrance to your home may be the sole entry used by members of your household as well as guests, or it may only be used by guests and therefore overlooked since you aren't walking through it each morning and evening. Taking note of how the entryway is used and considering the space from other points of view will help you figure out the specific pieces that the space requires.

Furnishing your entryway can break up a long hallway and give the area a purpose. It also gives you the opportunity to display family photos and other favourite pieces. You might add a console table by the door that provides a home for keys, mail and other items you arrive home with.

Entryways

HOME

Front doors

First impressions count—we're told not to judge a book by its cover but it's hard not to do this when it comes to imagining what may lie beyond the front door. Your front door is a teaser for your guests, a hint of what's to come when the door opens, so there's no need to make it serious and boring. Adding some personality and character that reflects you and your family is the perfect way to hint to your guests that the rest of the home is a stylish habitat.

Making over your front entrance doesn't need to cost the earth. A weekend spent painting is often all you require to make a bold statement. Some new entry lights, a potted plant and a snazzy doormat are relatively inexpensive pieces that can transform the space in seconds. If the period of your home calls for it, installing some faux shutters either side of your front windows adds instant architectural interest to the front of your home.

When lighting your front door, consider who will use this entry in the evenings. Will you be coming home from after-school activities in the dark with lots of school bags, tripping over the garden as you approach, or are your guests the only ones to use this entry? Lighting the pathway with solar-powered lights allows you to see where you're stepping, while a lovely big pendant light hanging in the entryway adds an elegant touch. Also consider hanging some wall sconces either side of your front door. These can be as plain or decorative as you like as long as they provide an inviting glow.

Don't forget about the vegetation. Greenery and flowers planted around your front door will add character and colour to your entryway. The flowers bring a pop of colour to the area, while greenery adds some lovely texture and gives the home a lived-in and loved look. If you're short on garden space, consider two large potted plants either side of your front door. Citrus plants make great potted plants in this area because they provide greenery as well as a hint of colour when in fruit.

Entryway basics

Your entryway may be the smallest area of your home but it is probably the most frequently used in terms of traffic flow, so selecting sturdy pieces will serve you well. Your decorative choices will stand the test of time if you choose multifunctional pieces.

Below is a list of the items that are most typically used for entryways, but you don't need all of them. Choosing what works best for you and your home is the key. Consider:

- console table or cupboard
- armchair
- table lamps
- pendant light
- hall runner
- rug
- hooks.

DECORATOR'S TIP

Lighting a scented candle in your entryway adds a welcoming touch for guests.

Entryways

HOME

Applying the elements of decorating to the entryway

NEEDS + WANTS

Think about what you need in your entryway and what you want to regularly use there. Who uses the space and for what activities? Do you require an area for shoes? Do you come in the front door and dump your keys and mail on the table and never tidy them up again? What if you had a storage trunk for kids' shoes and a drawer in the hall table dedicated to mail and keys—would it encourage you to keep the area neat and tidy?

For your entryway, consider small storage and shoe storage to keep the area tidy, hall runners or doormats to trap dirt, and table lamps to provide mood lighting. You might also position a chair near your entry console so your guests have a spot to take their shoes on and off. An armless chair will take up little space, while also providing a handy function.

COLOUR + PATTERN

When choosing the three to five colours for your entryway, you need to look at whether any other rooms are visible from this area. If so, the colour palette in the entryway will need to reflect the colour palette in those rooms. You can add colour and pattern to the entryway with:

- rugs
- a lampshade
- a bright tray
- hand-painted artwork
- a gallery wall of family photos
- wallpaper
- candles
- an occasional chair
- a stack of books
- flowers.

Although the entryway may be a small and multifunctional space, it doesn't deserve any less attention than other parts of your home. A narrow or small area can present some decorating issues but that's all the more reason to put on your creative thinking cap and come up with some solutions.

Consider the shape and size of the hall or entry itself. Are there already a lot of linear lines with the doorways, hallways and a rectangular console table? One way to break up these straight, harsh lines is to add some rounded shapes. For example, place a circular rug on the floor instead of a long hall runner or hang a round mirror above the console table (not only is a mirror useful for last-minute touch-ups before you head out the door, it can also reflect a nice view from a nearby window and add a little extra natural light to the space). Another option for contrasting the linear lines is to hang hooks on the walls for coats, bags and hats. The hooks also keep your everyday items neatly stored and ready for use.

PLACEMENT

Traffic flow is an extremely important factor to consider when deciding on furniture placement in the entryway. If the space allows, a round rug with a round table centred to the room makes an elegant statement as you enter—but you will need to allow for ease of movement around the table. If you're short on space, a narrow rectangular console table is a better use of space and means you can place a few decorative objects on top without encroaching on the pathway to the next room. Don't forget to consider the doorways, as these will affect your furniture options, too.

Your table of choice will unintentionally become the focal point of your entryway if it is left undecorated. If you would prefer that wasn't the case, you can use art or a beautifully framed mirror above the console or buffet to draw attention up and away from the table.

LIGHTING

Some ambient accent lighting in the entryway, rather than downlights blazing away, will do a better job of getting your guests in the mood for a sophisticated dinner party. You can achieve an inviting atmosphere by using a table lamp with a low-wattage bulb on your entry table. Two lamps make for a symmetrical and chic statement at the front door as well as providing ample lighting in the evening.

Entryways

HOME

3

Living rooms

Living room
decorating

The living room is typically the most used space in the home. It's also a common place for your family, flatmates or guests to congregate, so it often ends up being a multifunctional space. Even if you live alone, your living room will serve two main purposes: a space for you to entertain friends and a space in which you can relax.

The living room is the one room in your house that is left wide open to creative interpretation, as your furniture options are vast. Unlike a dining room, where the options are really only a table and chairs with a few other decorative pieces, the living room can have any number of different configurations. There may well be a number of fixtures that you still have to accommodate as well as walkways to consider but, overall, the living space has the most decorating flexibility. For example, there is a growing trend to focus more on cosying up the living room, making it into a retreat-like space and creating nooks within larger living spaces.

Your living room should be a room you are truly proud of. It may be the only room in your home that guests see because it's where you do your entertaining, so having a welcoming and personalised space is key.

Living room basics

Ottomans make a nice coffee table option in place of another timber element. They provide an opportunity to inject more colour, pattern or texture into the living space. Use a large tray (or two) to display and hold the typical coffee table items and to provide a sturdy place to rest a glass of wine in the evening.

Pieces that can be used to furnish a living room include:

- sofa
- chaise
- modular sofa
- armchair
- ottoman
- coffee table
- side table
- table lamp
- floor lamp
- pendant light
- rug.

Living rooms

HOME

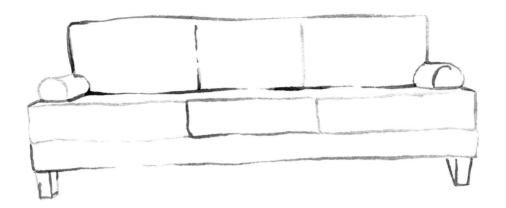

BUYING A SOFA

Your sofa will be one of the most used items in your living room. When buying a sofa, invest in quality and you'll be repaid in comfort for years to come. Here are some factors to consider.

Good bones: Look for a classic shape that won't go out of date.

Inside and out: Foam feather wraps are the best option for seat cushions. They'll hold their shape and you won't be forever fluffing them up before sitting down. A sofa with piped edges conveys a sense of luxury.

Do the maths: Consider your hallways and doorways. Don't just go for the biggest sofa option—it may not fit down the hall!

Living rooms

HOME

Living room focal points

In some cases living rooms can have more than one focal point, which can make decorating the room rather tricky. The three most common focal points for a living space are the TV, the fireplace and a window with a beautiful view.

In order to decide on the best furniture layout for a room with multiple focal points, you'll need to think about what you want as the primary focus. Do you want to have a conversational focus? Having your sofa and armchairs facing each other will help achieve this. Or is your living room centred around television viewing? Consider if it's possible to combine two focal points in one. For example, could the TV be hung above the fireplace?

The trends of incorporating a media room into the floor plan and of eating meals in living spaces mean formal dining rooms are being replaced and forgotten in many homes. We are now placing more importance on entertainment in our living spaces than we did in previous decades. Serving food in living spaces is also a regular occurrence.

The rise in popularity of media rooms also means that the TV inadvertently becomes the focal point in the room. But how do you disguise a TV if you don't want it to be the focal point? There are a number of options. Placing the TV in the corner of the room rather than front and centre means it doesn't compete for your attention as soon as you sit down. Or you can opt for a TV with a mirror finish so that when it's turned off you have a large mirror above your fireplace instead of a large black box. Alternatively, if you aren't much of a TV watcher, use a piece of art on a stretched canvas that you can slot over the top of your TV when it's not in use.

When styling a small space, use furniture with elevated legs to add breathing space between the floor and the item of furniture. Pieces that sit on the floor can look imposing and make the space feel cramped.

Living rooms

HOME

Furniture layouts + floor plans

Furniture placement will dictate how the living room is used. It can impact on the flow of conversation when entertaining, the ease of TV viewing during a big sporting game, or how you enjoy family time when you're all gathered around the coffee table for pizza and a movie.

Here are a number of different layouts to consider that will either allow for easy conversation or enhance viewing pleasure, depending on your plans for the room. Page 64 shows layout options for when you need to incorporate a dining table into your living room.

CONVERSATIONAL FOCUS

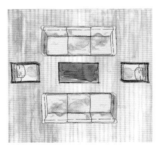
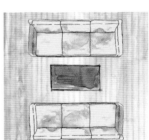

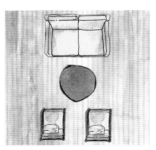

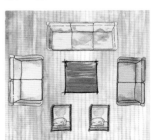

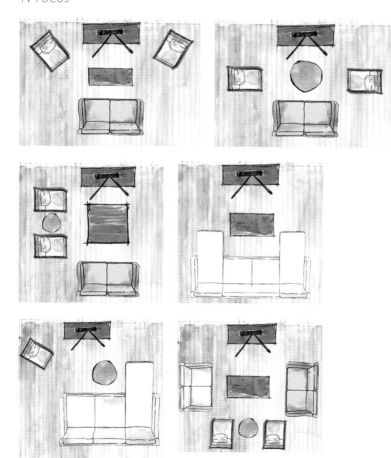

Living rooms

HOME

OPEN RECTANGULAR LAYOUT

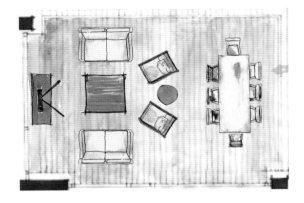

L-SHAPE LAYOUT

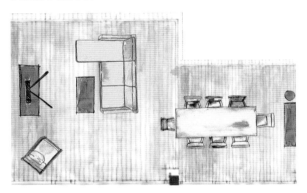

OPEN SQUARE LAYOUT

Adding life to your living room

Indoor plants are becoming more and more popular in homes, as they add an element that no furniture item or decorative object can: life!

Greenery can be used to fill a vacant corner of your living space. A tall indoor palm will add height and draw your eyes upwards, whereas something like a fiddle-leaf fig will fill out an empty space and provide depth of colour with its dark green leaves.

You'll notice that indoor plants are used in many magazines but they often only come part of the way into a photo. This styling trick means the plant helps fill the frame of the photo, without detracting or drawing attention from the intended focal point in the room. The same effect is achieved with landscaping around a house—it frames the exterior but doesn't dominate. You can easily use this trick in your own home if you have a green thumb. And if you feel you can't commit to a live plant, there are many fabulous imitation plants available to buy.

PLANTS SUITABLE FOR INDOOR USE

- Fiddle-leaf fig
- Dieffenbachia
- Mother-in-law's tongue
- Palms
- Maidenhair fern
- Philodendrons
- Bromeliads

Living rooms

HOME

Sofa styling

The topic of sofa cushions is a controversial one in many households, with many people dismissing them as unnecessary items. However, any decorator will tell you that the cushions on your sofa make or break the style of your room.

Always go up a size when buying feather inserts. The cushions will be fuller and fluffier for much longer. Avoid polyester-filled inserts— they will be as flat as pancakes in no time and aren't very comfortable to snuggle into.

CUSHION PLACEMENT GUIDE

Framing your sofa with two square cushions at either end is the perfect place to start. You can then build on this by adding various shapes and sizes. A rectangular lumbar cushion in the middle of the sofa is a good option for adding pattern and mixing up the shapes.

CUSHION OPTIONS

Cushion shapes are quite standardised. Below are some cushion combinations that work well on a sofa.

- Two 45 × 45 cm (18 × 18 in) cushions
- Four 45 × 45 cm (18 × 18 in) cushions
- Two 45 × 45 cm (18 × 18 in) + one 35 × 65 cm (14 × 25 in) cushions
- Two 55 × 55 cm (22 × 22 in) cushions
- Two 55 × 55 cm (22 × 22 in) + two 45 × 45 cm (18 × 18 in) cushions

Living rooms

HOME

Art placement

The wall behind a sofa is the greatest place for a statement in any living room. You may have a window behind your sofa, making the view out the window the focus for that wall. However, if you're faced with a blank wall, you can use art to bring the wall to life. Choose from these options to display your art in a way that makes a strong statement.

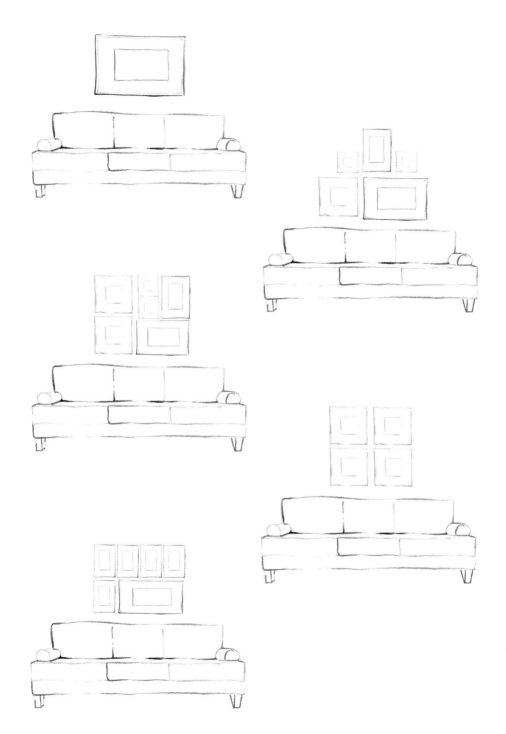

Living rooms

HOME

Applying the elements of decorating to the living room

NEEDS + WANTS

The living room is possibly the room with the most uses, so allowing for different needs and wants is important. Children will use a living space very differently to the adults in the house so it's vital that the space works for more than one purpose. List all the activities that occur in the living space and work out how best to accommodate each one. Perhaps your room is a playroom during the day, with toys strewn from one end to the other, but in the evening it's a relaxing space where you and your partner can unwind with a glass of wine and dinner at the coffee table. Being aware of the needs and wants of all the people who use the space will allow you to plan a useful and functional living space for everyone.

COLOUR + PATTERN

DECORATOR'S TIP

Mirrored furniture pieces, such as side tables or console tables, are excellent additions to darker living spaces. They reflect colour and pattern around the room and also add some additional light.

Your living space allows you to make the ultimate decorating statement, using colour and pattern around the room. When deciding on colours to use, stick to the rule of three to five colours, with your big-ticket items such as sofas and armchairs in relatively neutral colours for longevity. If you're feeling daring and want to use pattern on your upholstered pieces, the general rule of thumb is to go for a smaller print on larger items and reserve the large-scale patterns for items such as cushions. Large-scale patterns are confusing on large pieces; you can see smaller patterns much more clearly when they are used on an expansive space. Plain fabrics with texture are better choices for large upholstery as they'll allow for greater flexibility in the future and you can switch focal points without the sofa dominating each time.

SHAPE + SIZE

The living room is likely to house more furniture than any other room in your home, so planning your shapes and sizes will go a long way towards creating a visually pleasing space. Varying the amount of linear lines with some curved, softer edges will assist in making the space more inviting and relaxing. A round coffee table is ideal for children to play around during the day because they won't be bumping into sharp edges. Don't forget that lighting can add to the mix of shapes and sizes—a tall floor lamp will fill a dead corner and a tall table lamp on your side table will add visual height to the space.

PLACEMENT

Traffic flow and how the room is used will impact greatly on the placement of your furniture. If there are multiple entry and exit points to the room, your furniture will need to accommodate them. Is there a natural path for traffic flow or will the placement of your furniture help to dictate this? Often you'll need a few attempts to get the placement right, but planning ahead by making a floor plan will help considerably. See pages 62–64 for some living room floor plan options.

LIGHTING

Mood lighting in the living room is the aim. Varying your lighting options is the fastest way to create a lovely atmosphere. Installing dimmer switches for your downlights allows you to control the level of light. Add a few well-placed table or floor lamps and a grouping of candles on your coffee table and you'll have a perfectly lit room.

DECORATOR'S TIP

Neutral upholstery can be tricky. The best way to avoid a dark, den-like living space is to vary the taupe brown shades and avoid selecting fabrics too close to the colour of your timber pieces.

Don't match your sofa fabric with your armchair fabric—too much of one colour in an expansive space isn't such a good thing. Break it up with a pattern on the armchair for a stand-out statement piece or go a few shades darker or lighter than the sofa for contrast.

Living rooms

HOME

4

Dining rooms

Dining room decorating

The name 'dining room' implies that there is only one use for this room. But more often than not, the dining table serves many purposes, from a place to enjoy dinners with friends to somewhere to help children with their homework; it can even function as a home office desk space. The dining room may get overlooked on weeknights when we'd prefer to plop down on the sofa and watch TV while eating dinner. But when it comes to entertaining, the room is transformed into a congregational space where meals are eaten and stories are shared until late into the evening.

No longer do we have a formal dining room and a casual dining room—in many homes, they have merged into one space. This is especially true in large, open-plan spaces where there are three rooms combined into one and having another separate, more formal eating area seems a waste of space. This trend of open-plan living means that the dining room is now more like the dining area of a multifunctional space.

Typically, the dining table should be placed nearest to the kitchen exit point, especially if the dining area is part of an open-plan space. This saves you from carrying meals through the living space and potentially tripping over rugs and furniture.

Dining rooms

HOME

Dining room basics

DECORATOR'S TIP

If you're short on space, select dining chairs that don't have arms, giving you the most seating space around your dining table. Chunky arms take up vital dining table real estate.

Pieces that can be used to furnish a dining room include:

- dining table
- dining chairs
- carver chairs
- buffet
- sideboard
- hutch
- console table
- glass display cabinet
- bar cart
- floor lamp
- rug.

CHOOSING A DINING TABLE

Your choice of dining table will instantly dictate the style of the room. For example, a long, rustic, timber table suggests long conversations over informal family dinners, whereas a glass-topped metal table creates a slick, modern look that is more suited to a bachelor pad in an urban loft apartment.

There are several choices of materials for dining tables.

Timber: Choosing sturdy timbers such as walnut, oak, teak or pine will ensure longevity.

Metal: For an industrial look, opt for a powder-coated table that can even withstand being used outdoors.

Glass top: These are easily wiped down and won't show wear and tear as fast as a timber table will. Glass-topped tables are a great solution for small dining rooms—they aren't imposing and they allow you to show off a fabulous floor rug.

MDF: This is an inexpensive version of a solid timber table, yet has the same warm look as timber.

Check whether the table will be assembled before shipping. If the manufacturer ships the table unassembled, the tools you need to assemble it will usually be included. However, it's always wise to check you have what you need so that you don't have to make an emergency trip to a hardware store.

Furniture layouts
+ floor plans

It goes without saying that the table is the largest stand-out piece to work around in the dining room, and it takes central position at all times. Dining tables usually come in one of four shapes. The illustrations below show the best layout for each of these four table types.

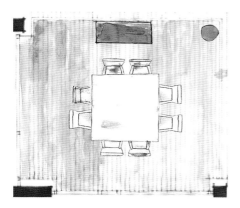

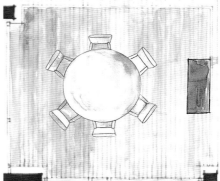

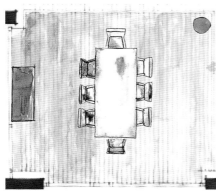

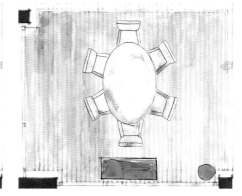

Dining storage

If your space allows, the dining room is the perfect place for overflow storage of anything that won't fit in your kitchen cupboards. There are various storage options, even for small rooms. Choose the maximum amount of storage that your room will allow.

STORAGE OPTIONS FOR THE DINING ROOM

Buffet: A long cabinet, typically featuring four doors that you can close to house your overflowing teacup collection.

Sideboard: A longer version of the buffet that typically features a mix of doors and drawers, making it ideal for storing cutlery and glassware.

Hutch: A tall cabinet with a mix of drawers and glass-fronted doors. You can also store and display your special crockery and dinnerware in a hutch, rather than hiding it behind cupboard doors.

Console table: A great addition to a narrow dining room, as it's slim yet functional. Use the top of your console to display some trinkets.

Glass display cabinet: A special place to keep all your treasures locked out of harm's way. Make sure you dust it regularly, as there are a lot of reflective surfaces to give away your cleaning habits.

Floating shelves: Shelves that can be hung between windows or on their own as a feature on the wall. These are great for small spaces. Make sure you keep the shelves neatly arranged and free of dust, as they are always on display.

Bar carts: A bar cart is the ultimate dining room storage cabinet. Bar carts range in materials from timber to metal. They make an excellent storage feature where you can have fun arranging your favourite liquors and cocktail glass collection.

Tray
Champagne bucket
Ice tongs
Bottle opener
Pourer
Shot measure
Strainer
Shaker
Swizzle sticks
Napkins

Dining rooms

79

Applying the elements of decorating to the dining room

Think about how you use your dining room. Is the area going to be a multifunctional space where kids do homework in the afternoons and family meals are served in the evenings? Do you regularly host long, elaborate dinner parties, meaning bench-style seating would be uncomfortable? Would it be handy to gain some additional storage space for the cutlery and china you inherited from your grandmother? Do you have young children who regularly drop their dinner scraps on the floor, making a nice rug underneath your table an impractical addition to the room?

COLOUR + PATTERN

Considering a dining area has relatively few items in it, choosing colour and pattern is a delicate decision. Typically the largest item in the dining room is the table. Timber, metal and glass tables all tend to be neutral, which can limit your options for adding colour and pattern. Instead, you can choose bold-coloured chairs or jazzy seat cushions, a patterned rug, bright curtains or funky lampshades. Don't forget that you can have fun with your dining table centrepiece, as well as the art on the walls.

SHAPE + SIZE

If you're the type to fall in love with furniture pieces and buy them with little thought or consideration for what will actually fit in your space, things could go horribly wrong for you in the dining room. You may be able to get away with that kind of buying behaviour in a bedroom or kid's playroom, but the dining room is a strict and unforgiving room when it comes to furniture size. Your room should dictate the size of your table, but it often pays to think outside the box. You don't have to buy a rectangular table simply because the room is rectangular. Mixing up linear lines creates interest, so an oval-shaped dining table will provide a nice contrast. The same applies in a square dining room—placing a round dining table often results in a more pleasing outcome for the space.

DECORATOR'S TIP

Allow about 50–70 cm (20–28 in) push-back space for your dining chairs.

Dining rooms

HOME

PLACEMENT

It goes without saying that the dining table will be the first piece placed in the room. Typically it is centrestage, as well as the focal point for the dining room. Traffic flow is of extreme importance in this space. Think about and allow for the natural flow of foot traffic. Are there various entry and exit points? Do you walk into the room from the kitchen and continue moving through it to the living room? The entry and exit points will often dictate where your table is placed. A table with rounded edges will help considerably with ease of movement.

LIGHTING

When considering your dining room lighting options, do your homework. Think about the lighting in your favourite restaurants. Do you sit in artificial light that is reminiscent of a hospital waiting room, or does some moody, atmospheric lighting help make dining an enjoyable experience? Replicating this experience in your own home is actually much easier than it sounds. All you need to do is install a dimmer switch for your overhead lighting (downlights or a pendant centred to the table). It is not expensive to have an electrician do this and it allows you more control over the way the room is lit in the evening. Next it's simply a matter of layering your lighting by adding a floor lamp in a corner of the room or placing a table lamp on top of a buffet or sideboard. Also consider wall sconces—the light will wash gently up the walls, adding to the moody feel.

Entertaining friends

Tablecloth
Placemats
Napkins
Dinner ware
Serving ware
Cutlery
Water glasses
Water jug
Champagne or wine glasses
Wine carafe
Coasters
Place cards
Salt and pepper shakers
Decorative centrepiece

Formal dining setting

Dinner parties are the perfect excuse to break out the good cutlery and dinner ware. You'll usually find a linen napkin for formal dining, with three sets of cutlery—one set for the entree, one for the main course and one for dessert. Your selection of plates will match your cutlery options. As for glasses, the choices are water, red wine or white wine glasses. If you're ever a guest at a formal dining experience and are confused about which utensil to use for what, simply start from the outside and work your way in. The cutlery on the outside is for the entree and the cutlery closest to the plate is for the main course. The cutlery above your plate is for dessert.

Casual dining setting

Less is more when it comes to items used for casual dining. Typically you will only need one set of cutlery with a dinner plate, entree plate, water glass, wine glass and a paper napkin. Everyone's definition of casual varies, though; sometimes casual dining means finger food, negating the need for cutlery or even plates.

Dining rooms

HOME

5

Bedrooms

Bedroom decorating

Your bedroom should be your hideaway, your tranquil oasis and your relaxing sanctuary. However, the master bedroom is often overlooked in favour of furnishing the living and dining rooms. It's easy to see why—typically your bedroom is only seen by you, your significant other, family members or housemates. Why bother investing in it when hardly anyone enters the room? The answer is: for your own happiness and relaxation.

We spend roughly one third of our lives asleep, yet the bedroom isn't only reserved for sleeping. Plenty of other activities take place in the bedroom, from reading and having breakfast to planning your next holiday and other activities. Since you spend so much time in your bedroom, it makes sense to spend some time decorating and styling the space to your taste.

Even though the bedroom can be a multifunctional space, it's important to ensure the room is very clearly a place for relaxing and unwinding. It's not a place for working or overstimulating yourself with technology.

Most people have strong feelings on the topic of TVs in the bedroom. If you do have a TV in your bedroom, don't let it dominate as the focal point of the room. Perhaps opt for a small-screen TV that hides behind sliding cupboard doors when it's not in use or sits at the side of the room so it's not so obvious.

Bedroom basics

Pieces that can be used to furnish a bedroom include:

If you want to inject some humour and fun into your bedroom decor, mismatched bedside tables will add a quirky touch. Make sure they still complement each other—two very different styles can clash and result in an eclectic disharmony.

- bed
- bedside table
- bed ottoman
- wardrobe
- chest of drawers

- desk
- chair
- armchair
- bedside lamp
- rug.

Furniture layouts
+ floor plans

The shape of your room will dictate the bed placement to a certain extent. Ideally, the bed should be placed with the head against the wall you face when you enter the room. That will make the focal point a beautifully made bed or patterned bedhead, rather than the side of the bed. Here are some layout options for your bedroom.

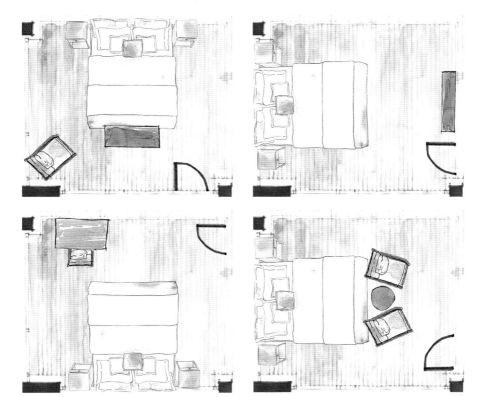

Types of beds

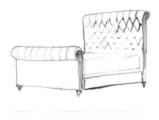

If your house isn't blessed with built-in cupboards, you can add some hidden storage. Consider an under-mattress drawer, a gas-lift bed with storage underneath or an ottoman with a removable lid (perfect for storing winter blankets and linens).

There are a number of different types of beds to consider.

Ensemble base: A plain base mimicking the look of the mattress quilting. A valance will add class to an ensemble base and a bedhead is the ultimate accessory to dress it up.

Base + frame: A simple bedding option with a built-in bedhead and surrounding frame, usually made from timber or upholstered in a sturdy fabric.

Sleigh: Typically a large, sturdy bed frame with a curved timber bedhead and matching timber base.

Four-poster: A stately bedroom option with all four bedposts rising up towards the ceiling. Often material (such as a mosquito netting) is draped over the top of the bedposts to form a canopy, adding an elegant touch.

BEDROOM LINEN

If you want to create a luxe hotel feel, invest in quality linen and layer it with soft furnishings. Lush fabrics to layer include vintage-wash linen sheets, sheepskin cushions, cashmere throw rugs and plush carpet.

The easiest option for bed linen is white. White is also the most luxurious looking, as long as you bleach it when you wash it—dull white sheets scream, 'No one cares!' Use decorative scatter cushions and a coloured or patterned throw rug or doona cover to inject colour instead.

For a more relaxed look, opt for cottons and linens rather than velvets and sheepskins. Mismatched cushions add to the relaxed look, so vary the size of scatter cushions you use to give off a casual feel. If you're the type to leave your bed unmade, run with this theme by pulling the doona over and throwing some scatter cushions haphazardly on the bed. This solves the hassle of making a pristine bed each morning!

Styling your bed

A beautifully made bed doesn't have to take half of your morning to put together. Follow the ingredients list and the steps below to achieve a perfectly made bed.

INGREDIENTS

European pillows
Standard pillows
Decorative cushions
Sheets
Doona
Throw rug

Place two European pillows against the bedhead or wall. Then sit the standard pillows in front of the European pillows, and the decorative cushions in front of the standard pillows. Use whatever configuration you like best for the decorative cushions—perhaps matching pairs or a trio of different sizes and shapes. Fold the sheets back over the top of the doona. To finish off the look, drape a throw rug over the end of the bed.

BEDROOM CUSHION GLOSSARY

- European pillows: 60 × 60 cm (24 × 24 in)
- Standard pillows: 50 × 65 cm (20 × 26 in)
- Decorative scatter cushions: 45 × 45 cm (18 × 18 in)
- Decorative lumbar cushions: 35 × 65 cm (14 × 26 in)
- Breakfast cushions: 50 × 80 cm (20 × 32 in)

OPTIONS FOR CUSHION EDGES

- **Knife edge:** No fancy trims, just straight edges joined at the seam.
- **Piped:** Self-piped in the same fabric as the pillow or contrast-piped in a different fabric.
- **Flange:** A thick, floppy fabric trim in the same fabric as the pillow.
- **Decorative trim:** Similar to piping but with fancy trims like pompoms or fringing.

Bedrooms

HOME

How do you decide how many cushions your bed needs? Take
a look at the illustrations below and pick which one you would
like to replicate in your bedroom.

Option 1

2 European pillows + 2 standard pillows +
2 decorative scatter cushions

Option 2

2 European pillows + 2 standard pillows +
1 decorative lumbar cushion

Option 3

2 European pillows + 2 standard pillows +
2 decorative scatter cushions + 1 decorative lumbar cushion

Option 4

4 standard pillows + 1 decorative lumbar cushion

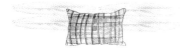

Option 5

4 standard pillows + 2 decorative scatter cushions

Option 6

2 European pillows + 2 standard pillows +
3 decorative scatter cushions

Bedroom feature walls

There are so many areas of the bedroom you can choose to make a feature of, from the bed linen to the bedhead to a feature armchair. However, if you're feeling really bold, a feature wall is a great way to unleash your creativity.

OPTIONS FOR FEATURE WALLS

- Wallpaper
- Painted feature wall
- Grouping of art (see 'Art 101' on page 176)
- Mirror
- Objet d'art

Bedside basics

Bedside tables are another place to show off your styling skills. Opt for a bedside table with drawers if you know you'll struggle to keep the top neat and free of clutter. For ease of use, the bedside tabletop should be roughly in line with the top of your mattress. Refer to the ingredients list for ideas on decorating your bedside tables.

Vase
Flowers
Ring dish
Tray
Candle
Picture frame
Books
Lamp
Ornaments
Alarm clock

Decorative object to fill the gap and make it more visually pleasing

Lamp for vertical height

Flowers for a touch of colour

Book stack for horizontal interest

Bedrooms

HOME

The guestroom

Double or queen bed
Bedside table
Bedside lamp
Water glass
Alarm clock
Extra blanket
Extra pillow
Dressing gown
Fresh flowers
Tissues
Bath towel and face cloth
Toothbrush and toothpaste
Shampoo and conditioner
Hand cream
Reading material
Notepad and pen
Candle
Matches
Coathangers
Tidy bin

When preparing your guestroom, think of a luxurious hotel visit and try to recreate that feeling for your guests—but obviously on a budget! The secret lies in the details, right down to hand cream and a toothbrush for the forgetful guest.

If you have the space available, clear out a little section of a cupboard so that your guests have somewhere to store their clothes if they are staying for more than one night. Make sure your guests know where to find everything you have prepared for them. There's nothing worse than waking up cold in the night and wondering where the spare blankets are kept.

Follow the ingredients list to ensure all your guests' needs are taken care of.

*Fresh flowers are a nice
welcoming touch in your
guestroom and show
your guest you've thought
through all the details
of their stay.*

Applying the elements of decorating to the bedroom

The majority of activities in the bedroom centre around the bed, so making the bed your main consideration when furnishing the room will assist in the decorating process. Bedroom needs and wants are relatively obvious. However, considering the needs and wants of your partner, who shares the bedroom, is a definite must. For example, your partner may like to read in bed and therefore need a reading lamp with an arched arm rather than a stick base. Stopping and thinking about specific details is key.

COLOUR + PATTERN

Subtle colours don't have to be dull and drab. Feel free to add colour and fun to your bedroom, but remind yourself that you want to feel a sense of calm when you enter, not have your eyes darting from one bright statement to the next. Keeping the large expanse of bed linen fuss free also enables you to achieve a sanctuary-like feel. Reserve colour and pattern for your scatter cushions and even your floor rug. If you do prefer colour and pattern on the bedspread, choose solid colours for your pillows and cushions so there are no pattern clashes.

You may have always wanted to sleep in a king-size bed but if the room doesn't allow for it you may have to settle for a queen-size bed. Play up the drama of the room with your bedhead. You can go for a tall, upholstered bedhead for a dramatic statement or opt for a neutral linen that sits just above your pillows for a more subtle look. It's also important to keep the height of the bed in mind. Don't pick a tall ensemble base if your ceilings are already feeling low; you'll benefit from a lower bed base, as it will make your ceilings feel higher.

PLACEMENT

The placement of your bed is paramount. There are all sorts of feng shui rules that apply to the placement of your bed, but ultimately it comes down to the size of the room and where your doorways and wardrobe are placed. A good guide is to sit your bedhead against the longest wall. If this is opposite the main entry door the proportions are spot on. Ideally you need around 60 cm (24 in) either side of the bed for getting in and out of bed easily.

LIGHTING

Of all the rooms in the house to benefit from a little extra thought when it comes to mood lighting, the bedroom is the most important. Dimmer switches are key, as are multiple light sources, such as table lamps or floor lamps. It's also important to consider whether you use your bedroom mirror when getting ready in the morning. If the natural light isn't sufficient, you'll need to ensure you have adequate overhead lighting.

Bedrooms

HOME

6

Home offices

Home office
decorating

If there is one room in every home that's guaranteed to be a wasteland of junk, paperwork and general untidiness, it's the home office or study. It's often the room that receives the least attention, which is counterintuitive considering that a room where we work, organise family life or pay household bills should be neat, organised and tidy.

A little thought and hard work goes a long way in the home office, especially when it comes to filing. Putting good systems and processes in place will mean your home office stays shipshape. Your first step is to consider the layout of the room and the best use of the space.

When it comes time to decorate your home office, the mix of functionality and design is important. If you select furniture that solves a variety of your storage and design needs, you'll enjoy a much tidier and more ordered room. Don't forget that the walls can be used for storage and organisation.

Home office basics

Pieces that can be used to furnish a home office include:

- desk
- chair
- lamp
- bookshelf
- filing cabinet
- other storage.

Styling
your desk

The key to a neat and tidy desk is organisation and planning, but you also need to consider the scale and balance of the items on the desk.

The lamp is usually the tallest item on the desk, so use that as your guide for where to place other items. A vase of flowers can also be tall, so you'll achieve a nice balance by placing this on the opposite side of the desk. Add smaller objects like a pencil tin and in-tray around these taller items. Hanging a pinboard above your desk gives you somewhere to pin unpaid bills and your 'to do' list, helping keep your finances and household tasks on track. Follow the ingredients list to make your own magazine-worthy desk display.

INGREDIENTS

Desk lamp
Clock
Computer
Mouse
Printer
Corkboard and pins
Storage boxes
In-tray
Rubbish bin
Writing paper
Pens and pencils
Ruler
Stapler
Sticky tape
Paperclips

Home offices

Storage

Sleek, well-placed storage will serve your home office needs for a long time and hopefully work for you as your family grows or your employment changes.

If you choose to install built-in cupboards anywhere in your home, it will add to the home's overall value. Built-in storage also provides you with ready-to-use storage space when you move in, which speeds up the unpacking process, especially when it comes to all those loose paperclips, pens and piles of paperwork.

If you can't commit to built-ins, freestanding open shelves are a great alternative. These can be moved from room to room as your storage needs change, and give you the space to style and showcase special objects to jazz up your home office. Open-shelf storage is the perfect option for renters, who can pack up the shelf and move it to the next home.

STORAGE OPTIONS

- Built-in cupboards
- Desk with built-in storage
- Filing cabinets
- Storage boxes
- Credenza
- Open storage

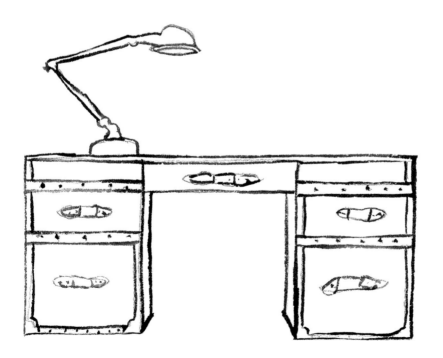

Applying the elements of decorating to the home office

Listing the specific activities that generally occur in your home office will help you identify what role the room plays and where to break up each activity within that room. Is the space a multifunctional room combining a desk, a pull-out sofa bed and your personal gym? Perhaps you could move the gym to the garage to free up some much-needed space to get your home office in working order. One of the most important functions of a home office is providing functional storage space. It may be the place where you house your second closet as well as your filing cabinet, so focusing on buying the right storage pieces is a good place to start.

COLOUR + PATTERN

Selecting a colour palette for your home office can be difficult because there are so many elements in the room to consider. Neutral walls work best as they won't compete for your attention all day long. Keep the desk and other furniture items neutral, too. This will also make them more versatile. Bring in colour and pattern with a fun desk-chair fabric, or cover your pinboard in a coloured fabric. Add some bright desktop accessories to show off your decorative talents.

Home offices

HOME

SHAPE + SIZE

If you are trying to squeeze a desk as well as a guest bed into your home office space, you need to consider the size of each piece to ensure you are using the area wisely. Write a wishlist of furniture you'd like for the room and then measure the space and make a floor plan to ensure it will all fit. You may have to compromise here and there but there is a storage solution to suit every need. You may just need to think outside the box in order to fulfil your furniture and storage wishes.

PLACEMENT

Your desk should take prime position—perhaps it's under a window, against a wall or centred to the room. Wherever you place your desk, the expanse of wall or window above it will need some attention in the way of artwork, curtains or a pinboard. Pinboards or inspiration boards are an ideal feature above a desk, serving a practical purpose as well as giving you a place to pin up pictures such as your children's artwork, photos or other images that inspire you.

LIGHTING

Task lighting is of utmost importance in a home office. To prevent eye strain, use a number of different light sources including natural light, table lamps and overhead lighting. If your overhead lights are too bright for daytime use, there will be considerable glare on your computer screen, so being able to vary the lighting (including adjusting natural light with curtains) is a must.

Don't have the space available to dedicate a whole room to your home office? Desk-friendly spaces can pop up anywhere in your home. Rethink an unused corner of your living room or a long hallway that might be just the right size for a small desk and chair.

Home offices

HOME

7

Nurseries + kids' bedrooms

Decorating nurseries + kids' bedrooms

Your child's nursery or bedroom needs to evoke a number of different feelings. Most importantly, it needs to help the child feel safe, cosy, serene and inspired. This room is the child's cocoon, a shelter from annoying siblings and a safe place to retreat to after a tiring day of play. We only get one chance at childhood, so why not make your child's room a special place that they will remember fondly for a lifetime?

Fitting out a nursery or a kid's bedroom doesn't have to cost you an entire year's salary. There are plenty of cheap and cheerful ways to decorate a child's bedroom—it's just a matter of prioritising purchases and doing your homework. Plus, your kids may not have inherited your expensive taste just yet so they'll be happy with chain-store purchases or homemade items. Most importantly, have fun with the decor in your kids' rooms and allow them to express their own personalities through it.

Nursery basics

*Buy furniture you'll be able to use for years to come.
Is a change table really necessary? Or could your chest of drawers double as a change table if you place a padded change mat on top?*

Pieces that can be used to furnish a nursery include:

- cot
- change table and change pad
- nursing chair
- chest of drawers
- storage baskets
- lamp
- rug.

It's worth doing your research before choosing a nursing chair. Below are some factors to consider before you make a purchase.

Low arms: *Being able to hold the baby without having your elbows pushed up against your body is vital. Choose a chair with low arms so that you have somewhere to support your arms while feeding the baby, but make sure your arms aren't so uncomfortably high that you're forced to sit on the edge of the armchair.*

High back: *Having a spot to rest your head during night-time feeds is crucial.*

Rocking: *Trying to rock bub to sleep in a regular armchair is close to impossible. A rocking function will save you from many hours of standing up and swaying.*

Footstool: *Chances are, you'll be in this chair at all hours of the day and night, so having somewhere to pop your feet up will be a little luxury.*

Quality: *Investing in a quality chair will see you through several babies.*

Multifunctional: *Can you use the nursing chair as an armchair in your living room when bub grows up?*

Decorating before baby arrives

Incorporating hand-me-downs can be tricky. Consider whether you can repaint the piece so that it fits with your nursery theme.

Decorating a nursery without knowing whether your baby is a boy or a girl is entirely possible and not difficult. Ensure the big-ticket items such as the cot, nursing chair and change table are all relatively neutral in colour. Choose colours such as pastel yellow, mint green, greys, taupes or even teal.

Once the baby arrives you can add a fourth or fifth colour that relates to the baby's gender. This will also allow for an inexpensive accent change if your next baby is a different gender.

Choosing a theme for the nursery can be an agonising task. Some lovely ideas include:

- circus animals
- safari
- nautical
- princess grandeur
- Scandinavian minimalism
- adventurer.

Nursery furniture layouts + floor plans

If you haven't planned ahead and worked out a rough floor plan for your nursery, stepping into a nursery furniture store can be overwhelming. The most important pieces in a nursery are the cot and change table. Start by placing these pieces and you'll find the decisions about where to put other items, such as a nursing chair, floor lamp and bookshelf, will fall into place. The nursery layouts below will give you some ideas.

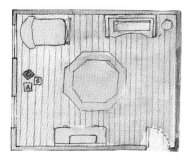
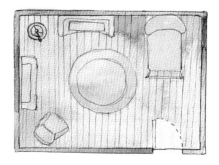

Kids' bedroom basics

Pieces that can be used to furnish a kid's bedroom include:

- bed
- trundle bed
- bedside table
- desk
- chair
- armchair
- laundry basket
- lamp
- rug.

Storage options include:

- wardrobe
- chest of drawers
- toy chest
- open shelves
- baskets
- hooks and hangers
- under-bed drawers.

Kids' bedroom furniture layouts + floor plans

As a bed is typically the largest piece of furniture in a kid's room, it's vital that you place it in the best position for the space. Once this has been done, it's easier to identify where the other items in the room should go.

Many items for kids' rooms can be bought at chain stores. However, if you want the furniture to last, think about investing in a few quality pieces, such as the bed, mattress, chest of drawers, desk and rug, to see your kids into their teen years.

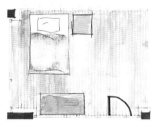
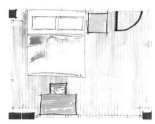

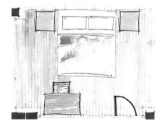
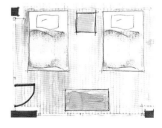

Girls vs. boys

Most people fall into one of two categories when it comes to decorating their child's bedroom. There are those who embrace it completely, unleashing their inner child and going wild with colour and themes, and there are those who are completely overwhelmed and end up with an underdone or lacklustre space.

It's tricky to get the right mix of fun and colour without falling into the land of cutesy characters and cartoons. If you plan on living in your home for several years, it's wise to make design and decor choices that will carry your child into their teen years, or tween years at the very least. Once you've invested your money, time and energy into decorating the room, you probably won't want to do it again a couple of years down the track.

As with the other rooms in your home, a neutral base will give you many colour and decor choices. It may sound hard to create a room that has a timeless, classic look that's injected with your child's personality, but the strategy of combining splurges and saves will serve you well. The idea is that you update the 'saves' every few years, while your 'splurges' remain sturdy investment pieces for many years. Once the neutral 'bones' are in place, you can then style according to your child's gender and personality.

GIRLS

The princess look is a popular choice, but trying to keep this mature and glamorous can be difficult. This is where your choices as an adult will ensure the room's decor lasts. Instead of picking wallpaper in pink and purple patterns, opt for gold or silver metallic patterns. This will add effervescence to the room but won't scream princess pink.

Choose an armchair or a love seat covered in a soft, velvety fabric that exudes luxe and sophistication. The cushions you place on the chair can be appropriate for your daughter's age, but in a couple of years you can change the look of the room by selecting new cushions, meaning you won't have to re-cover the entire chair.

BOYS

There are many themes that boys love to explore, such as superheroes, pirates and racing cars, but incorporating those themes without ending up with a tacky room can be a challenge. Sticking to the same rules as for girls will pay off. Choosing more adult-like pieces of furniture for the space will save you money in the long run.

For example, you can easily integrate a pirate or superhero theme by keeping the themed items to a minimum. A well-placed cushion with a skull and crossbones, black-and-white-striped curtains or a canvas artwork of a superhero all hint at a theme, while the rest of the decor is sophisticated and chic. A racing-car theme can be treated the same way; framing a selection of your son's matchbox cars in shadow boxes, adding a car-shaped rug or hanging vintage posters of famous race cars are all classy ways to incorporate the theme—no racing-car beds needed!

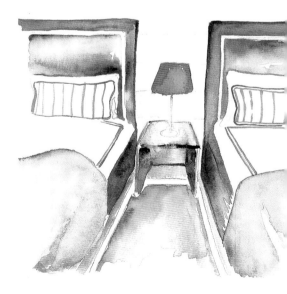

Siblings sharing a bedroom

Cohabitating with a sibling is hard work. It means you have to share more and compromise more—and you fight more. For parents, trying to work with two demanding 'clients' who want the exact opposite of each other can be a difficult task. The key is to designate each child a certain section of the room. This means that the children can clearly show off their own style without encroaching on their sibling's side. Ultimately, however, there will need to be some compromise so that the styles are somewhat complementary.

Consider using built-in shelving units to clearly demarcate each child's space. The shelves will also allow each child to display special trinkets and personalise their side of the room further.

If involving each child in the decorating process proves too trying, opting for a neutral colour scheme for the furniture and walls is probably best. Then allow the children to choose their own bed linen, night lights and bedside tables to personalise their areas.

If you don't have the floor space available to have two separate areas for the beds, using bunk beds is a good space-saving option. Placing the top bed perpendicular to the bottom bed is the best use of space, as it allows playing space below. This layout could also work well if the room is short on space and you need to incorporate a desk into the area. Instead of having a bed on ground level, you can have the bed up higher so there's space underneath for a built-in desk.

*To achieve a stylish kids' bedroom, go for
neutral colours for the permanent pieces. Keep
colour to the smaller, more mobile pieces like
bed linen, cushions, storage boxes and curtains,
and opt for more adult furniture pieces.*

Applying the elements of decorating to nurseries + kids' bedrooms

Practicality, functionality and durability are the three factors to consider when making buying decisions. Children aren't known to take good care of their bedroom furniture so durability should be at the top of your list. Price doesn't always reflect durability, so closely research your materials and their quality before making any decisions. Cheap impulse buys will end up costing you more in the long run.

Also consider that the needs and wants in kids' bedrooms will change much faster than in adults' bedrooms. It pays to think about the future before you make any purchasing decisions, and to invest where it makes sense. There are a growing number of children's furniture suppliers who manufacture transitional pieces that you can add to in order to get the most out of a piece of furniture. For example, there are cots that transform into toddlers' beds, which then transform into single beds. This means that you only make one large purchase at the beginning, rather than having to upgrade each time your child outgrows a bed. If you have more than one child, your furniture decisions will need to take into account your younger child and any potential future children. If you are investing in a cot for your first child, you want to be sure that it will last well into your future children's early years.

Placing items such as storage baskets and laundry baskets in your kids' bedrooms will ease your household duties. They will also encourage children to pack away their toys or put their dirty clothes in the laundry basket rather than dumping them on the floor. Of course, there are no guarantees that your child will use these baskets, but having them in place makes it more likely that they will put them to good use.

Don't forget to consult your child about their wants—after all, it's their space. For example, they may want a shelf or bedside table to display precious keepsakes—children collect many treasures and it's lovely for them to have somewhere special to display them. If you're feeling brave, why not allow your child to choose the colour palette, including the wall paint? If you seriously hate it, it's a relatively inexpensive element to change in a couple of years.

Make sure you leave some free space on the floor for playtime, particularly if your child is going to be using the bedroom for the majority of their activity time, rather than a dedicated playroom.

COLOUR + PATTERN

Decorating a kid's bedroom gives you full permission to have fun and splash colour everywhere. Applying the three-to-five colour rule often means that neutral colours don't get a look-in beyond the texture and materials of the furniture. Colour and pattern can have a significant impact on a child's behaviour and mood, making your colour choices all the more important.

So how do you use colour and pattern in kids' bedrooms? Bed linen is a great way to make a colourful statement without a long-term commitment. Another option is to wallpaper at least one wall—this is the perfect opportunity to add colour as well as pattern and make a big statement. It's important that your rug ties in with your linen and wallpaper choices, too. This could mean selecting a rug that has a similar colour tone to the wallpaper, or opting for complementary patterns in contrasting colours while still abiding by the three-to-five colour rule.

DECORATOR'S TIP

Keep your child's exposure to nasty chemicals to a minimum, especially in the bedroom. Opt for low-VOC (volatile organic compound) paints, solid timber materials, wool rugs and organic cotton or bamboo linens.

Nurseries + kids' bedrooms

HOME

When choosing fabrics for kids' rooms, durability is key. Slip covers will save your sanity (and your furniture, too).

If your child suffers from allergies, opting for low-shed materials that are as natural and organic as you can afford will help greatly.

Cotton: *This is versatile and comfortable for kids.*

Wool: *Naturally resistant to mould and mildew, wool is also non-allergenic.*

Linen: *Linen is strong and sturdy, as well as being breathable in summertime.*

Polyester blend: *This is a great choice for minimising wear and tear.*

Feature walls in children's bedrooms are extremely popular. There are a variety of options to allow you to create a striking effect, including wallpaper, paint, wall stickers and murals. However, you don't want to overstimulate your child, as they do need to unwind and relax in the room before bedtime. Keeping the decoration simple with a stripe or spot allows you to inject some fun without keeping your child awake at night.

SHAPE + SIZE

Many of your considerations here will be safety-related. For starters, making the best use of the space available for storage means it is inevitable that some items will be above easy reaching level. Be careful not to overfill drawers or storage baskets so children aren't pulling heavy drawers onto themselves. It's even worth considering using felt or rattan storage baskets that are kinder to little bodies than timber or metal.

Remember to look for furniture with rounded edges. Considering the rough-and-tumble play that can sometimes take place in kids' bedrooms, having a rounded edge to land on will hopefully mean fewer furniture-related injuries.

It's easy to go furniture shopping for kids' bedrooms and get caught up buying mini furniture items because they are cute or sweet, but don't fall into that trap with all your furniture decisions. It may be more beneficial to buy an adult-sized piece of furniture that can grow with your kids.

PLACEMENT

The floor plan of a child's bedroom is very different to that of an adult's bedroom. Typically, the majority of furniture is placed against the walls to keep the floor free for play. Built-in pieces can free up floor space; for example, a built-in desk that butts up against a bed or wardrobe is a good use of space. However, built-in pieces mean the room is locked in to that configuration, so be sure you are committing to the correct layout before your builders start work. Any large, fixed furniture pieces like drawers, chests and cabinets should be secured to the walls so that children can't pull the furniture onto themselves.

LIGHTING

Keep artificial lighting to a minimum and bring in as much natural light as possible. Harsh, direct sunlight isn't ideal, either. Use light-filtering options such as sheer curtains as well as blinds or heavier curtains to allow you to control the light levels, especially if your child is young enough to need a daytime nap.

Night lights should give off soft, warm light that helps put the child at ease if they wake up at night needing to use the bathroom or find the way to your room for reassurance after a bad dream.

If your child has a desk in the bedroom, good lighting will be a really important addition to the room. Don't forget a bedside lamp for reading bedtime stories!

Nurseries + kids' bedrooms

HOME

The playroom

If your children are lucky enough to have an entire room dedicated to play, a room that evokes fun, playfulness and creative freedom is perfect. Decorating a playroom doesn't need to be an expensive task. The colour palette alone can come from the toys the children use most. Ideally you want a space that they won't outgrow easily, but that is pleasing enough that you don't want to keep it hidden behind closed doors.

Setting up play stations around the room is great for keeping activities to dedicated spaces. For example, in an ideal world a craft table keeps arts and crafts in one spot, and empty floor space allows children to dance, fight ninja-style, build a fort or set up a picnic lunch. A dolls' house in the corner signifies that the doll collection lives in a particular area of the room.

In a playroom, storage is every parent's best friend. It's ideal to have different storage options so that you can house any and every toy, game or activity. It's always best to combine open and closed storage. Open shelving fulfils practical requirements and provides space for decorating with colourful tubs or your children's book collection. Closed options allow you to conceal mess. Varying your storage options with baskets, drawers, shelves and cabinets is perfect, as it means you can sort activities by drawer and encourage the children to put toys away in precise locations. Labelling the storage areas may be a fruitless effort if your children are too young to read. You may need to accept that it's better if they put toys away in any drawer than leave them strewn across the floor.

Durable and hardy furniture is a must for the playroom. You will only need a few pieces of furniture because the main activities will take place on the floor. If you're looking for a sofa for the

playroom, choose a wipeable fabric or even invest in a leather option that will serve you well over its lifetime. Opting for solid timber over MDF means any nicks or dents will just add to the timber's patina, so you don't have to worry about the furniture being ruined. Don't forget seating options, too. Moveable pieces, such as armchairs and beanbags, give more flexibility for race-track construction and provide handy seating for impromptu concerts.

The playroom is the one room in the house where the three-to-five colour rule can be broken. Chalkboard paint is available in a variety of colours beyond the classic black. Painting the walls in a coloured chalkboard paint will add a hit of colour and give your children a large surface on which to express their artistic talents. Another option is to install a felt bulletin board at your children's height, so they can display their artwork or educational items, such as maps and alphabet or number charts. Soft furnishings are another way to add variety to the colour palette.

Theming a playroom can be difficult if your children are sharing a space. Stick to incorporating individuality into their bedrooms and keep the playroom a neutral, fun space.

INGREDIENTS

Craft table
Sofa
Armchairs
Beanbags
Storage shelves
Storage cupboards
TV unit with storage
Rug

Nurseries + kids' bedrooms

HOME

8

Outdoor living spaces

Decorating outdoor living spaces

The outdoor area of your home is the ideal spot to create a little retreat from the world—a holiday nook where you and your family can escape on weekends or balmy summer evenings. This means the styling options for your outdoor living space are wide open to your imagination. If you want to create a relaxing, luxe island feel, go right ahead. If sophisticated Hamptons is more your style, this is your chance to let loose with nautical stripes and rope embellishments. Or perhaps you want to achieve a more rustic feel, with raw timber furniture and a fire pit for wintertime.

Outdoor spaces are usually the hub of our social activities in the summertime. Getting the decor right in these spaces can be tricky, especially since they are often a multifunctional space. You need to include areas for playing, eating and lounging, so some smart planning will pay off.

One thing that will always affect your outdoor decorating choices is the weather. Choosing hardy, weatherproof pieces may cost you more in the beginning but down the track you'll be rewarded with long-wearing, sturdy furniture that will endure the test of time.

HOME

Outdoor living + dining

The process for decorating your outdoor living space is similar to the process for decorating your indoor living space. In fact, treating your outdoor area as another living space is the perfect way to go about decorating, as it will result in an inviting and comfortable space. However, outdoor pieces have to be carefully chosen to endure the battering they'll receive from being outside.

All-weather furniture is a smart investment; many manufacturers offer synthetic versions of traditional outdoor furniture materials. Perhaps you love the rattan look, but keeping rattan outdoors will send it mouldy in just weeks. Opt instead for the synthetic rattan pieces available through many outdoor furniture suppliers. The costs vary depending on quality, but these usually make for a good investment as they are lightweight and still have that classic wicker look. If you prefer a more modern look for your outdoor areas, marine-grade stainless steel furniture is a worthwhile investment. These pieces are designed and manufactured to meet marine standards, so they provide excellent longevity.

However, typical indoor living room pieces can still be used to style your space: think about rugs, cushions and art. Some of these pieces, such as cushions, should be brought indoors after each use because leaving them constantly exposed to the elements will shorten their lifespan considerably.

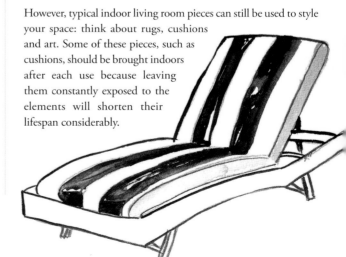

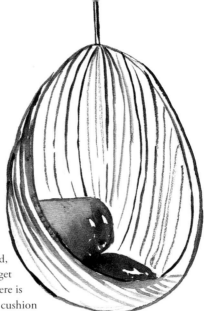

Even if your outdoor space is covered, you'll notice that fabrics fade faster or get damp during wet weather. Luckily there is a huge range of outdoor fabric and cushion insert material available for scatter cushions and sofa seat cushions. It's wise to do your homework before committing to bringing your cushions inside each time you use them.

As for rugs, there are a number of machine-made materials on the market that mean you can jazz up your outdoor flooring with some colour and texture. The two main options are plastic, usually made from recycled shopping bags or plastic drink bottles, and polypropylene, a synthetic resin. Both of these materials cope well with moisture and UV exposure.

To create a comfortable, welcoming spot to read a book in the afternoon sun or to relax after dinner, consider adding some daybeds. Daybeds are like permanent hammocks, ideal for siestas and lazy weekends. They also provide a great opportunity to add colour and pattern with bright, bold cushions.

Outdoor artwork is beginning to gain popularity. Advanced printing technology means that digital print canvases and digital prints on perspex can now be hung outdoors (but still undercover to protect them from the weather), thus allowing you to repeat your colour and pattern.

You can also bring your outdoor area to life with accessories, such as candle holders, table runners, placemats and small potted herbs. These are affordable items you can pop on the outdoor dining table or coffee table.

DECORATOR'S TIP

You may want to invest in some furniture covers if you know you won't be using your outdoor furniture regularly in winter. The covers will protect your furniture from the elements and also prevent fading, as the winter sun's rays can still cause fabric to fade.

Outdoor living spaces

HOME

Balconies

Balconies can vary greatly in size. Generally they are a place to entertain friends on sunny spring days or to enjoy family barbecues after a long week, so space for a dining table is ideal.

Small balconies limit your styling options but that doesn't mean you can't have fun with the space. Hanging pots, mini herb gardens and vertical gardens, as well as bright rugs and outdoor cushions, will all add character and spunk to your balcony.

Applying the elements of decorating to outdoor living spaces

NEEDS + WANTS

The area of your home that will be most affected by the seasons is your outdoor living area. In summertime we like to fling open the doors and live as though our outdoor space is an extension of our indoor living space. When the weather turns cooler, the doors are firmly shut and our outdoor spaces can become neglected and unloved. Being aware of the way you use this space year round will serve you well when buying furniture.

COLOUR + PATTERN

The architecture of your outdoor area and the natural surroundings will help dictate the style of your outdoor decor. Ultimately you can be a little playful with this area of your home, especially if you have children using the space. Choose a colour palette that will complement the exterior of your home, as that is the backdrop to your space and needs to be pleasing to the eye. The rest of the colour and pattern can be injected into your soft furnishings and rugs. If you have an indoor open-plan living area that leads to the outdoor living area, there should be some elements or colours that are repeated to tie the two areas together.

SHAPE + SIZE

Be aware of the space you have available and don't jam in as much furniture as the space will take simply so you can have a living and dining space in one. Think about how you will use the space most—will you be eating alfresco or lounging around more often? Deciding on one of the two will mean you can dedicate the whole space to that one activity rather than squeezing too many furniture items into the space and ruining the relaxed feel.

Outdoor living spaces

PLACEMENT

Breathing space in your outdoor area is vital. The back door is generally the only entry and exit point, but the surrounding yard probably means there are multiple walkways through the area. You need room to move and live in this area, and blocking traffic flow will affect how often you use it. Make movement in and around the area as convenient and fuss-free as possible and you'll spend all your free time there. Perhaps two armchairs will work better than one long sofa or vice versa, depending on the natural flow of traffic. Or maybe a smaller dining table and chairs are more suited to the space, allowing a larger area for lounging and relaxing.

LIGHTING

Entertaining in the summertime often means spending hours upon hours reclining or dining in the one area. Once the sun goes down, either the party breaks up or the lights go on so you can continue your fun into the evening. The main problem with lighting in an outdoor area is the bugs that are instantly drawn to the lights. Swapping your outdoor light globes for yellow tinted bulbs will aid in reducing bug numbers.

Varied lighting options are also important in your outdoor space. Pendant lights and wall sconces are ideal choices. It's a little tricky and also quite dangerous to have floor lamps and table lamps outdoors—you're better off leaving them indoors and bringing some citronella candles outside instead.

Outdoor living spaces

HOME

PLACEMENT

Breathing space in your outdoor area is vital. The back door is generally the only entry and exit point, but the surrounding yard probably means there are multiple walkways through the area. You need room to move and live in this area, and blocking traffic flow will affect how often you use it. Make movement in and around the area as convenient and fuss-free as possible and you'll spend all your free time there. Perhaps two armchairs will work better than one long sofa or vice versa, depending on the natural flow of traffic. Or maybe a smaller dining table and chairs are more suited to the space, allowing a larger area for lounging and relaxing.

LIGHTING

Entertaining in the summertime often means spending hours upon hours reclining or dining in the one area. Once the sun goes down, either the party breaks up or the lights go on so you can continue your fun into the evening. The main problem with lighting in an outdoor area is the bugs that are instantly drawn to the lights. Swapping your outdoor light globes for yellow tinted bulbs will aid in reducing bug numbers.

Varied lighting options are also important in your outdoor space. Pendant lights and wall sconces are ideal choices. It's a little tricky and also quite dangerous to have floor lamps and table lamps outdoors—you're better off leaving them indoors and bringing some citronella candles outside instead.

Outdoor living spaces

HOME

9

Styling

Styling your home

Once you have the basics of your rooms looking fabulous, you can commence the styling stage. Styling really refers to the placement of the more mobile pieces in the room and grouping them together in what is known as a vignette. This is your opportunity to create beautiful vignettes around your home, displaying items such as curios, mementos, knick-knacks and trinkets that you love and that hold significance for you and your family. These items can also become conversational pieces when guests are visiting your home.

Your goal when styling a vignette is to layer your trinkets and knick-knacks to tell various stories throughout the room. These stories aren't necessarily discovered at first glance. Only after spending an extended period of time in the room do you notice all its special features.

We all have items we have collected over the years that we don't quite know what to do with, such as not-so-treasured gifts or pieces your partner loves that you actually despise. Good homes for these items are the guestroom or powder room, where you won't often see them but you also won't have offended anyone by packing them away.

Styling

HOME

The five elements of styling

By now you will be very familiar with the elements that make up the decorating process, but there are different rules to follow when it comes to styling the finishing touches of the room.

This stage of the interior decorating process is definitely the most fun. It gives you the chance to experiment with your styling skills and to collate items you have collected throughout your life. By applying these five elements, you'll be able to piece together beautiful vignettes throughout your home.

1. TEXTURE

Texture provides visual weight to the overall look and style of the room. You can add texture with items made of velvet, hessian, linen, cotton or wool as well as timber. Most of the time it's a visual treat, but occasionally texture is only noticeable when you actually touch the object, making it all the more special. Neutral texture, when done well, can have just as much impact on a room as colour.

2. CONTRAST

Contrasting shapes within a vignette create balance and interest. Too many straight lines can feel clinical and boring. Mixing in some softer, rounded edges instantly offsets the harsh linear lines. For example, placing rounded objects on top of a rectangular tray is the perfect way to contrast the items in your vignette.

3. METALLICS

Metallic items are like jewellery for your home, adding sparkle and sophistication. Reflect the colour and other decorative elements in the room with metallic items such as a brass knob, a silver catch-all dish, a gold tray on a coffee table or a copper trinket on a bookshelf. You probably have a lot of these items around the house and finding a suitable place for them won't be hard at all.

4. LIFE

No room is complete without some greenery. Greenery adds life and texture to a room. Flowers, succulents and ferns are excellent additions to a vignette. They can also improve the quality of the air in your home. If you want to explore a more economical option, faux flowers in a vase can have the same visual impact as fresh flowers.

5. PLACEMENT

Placing your items within the vignette is often the trickiest part when it comes to putting your trinkets together. Taking a photo of the tray, shelf or area you're styling is a good way to help you identify anything that needs to be changed. An easy guide is to use repetition; for example, stack books or magazines rather than having one on its own.

DECORATOR'S TIP

You shouldn't attempt styling until the majority of the furniture and soft furnishings are in place. Once you're happy with the placement of the big-ticket items, you can commence styling.

Styling

HOME

The art of arranging

Lack of colour can be just as striking as a boldly coloured vignette. The key to making a neutral vignette work is to incorporate various interesting textures. For example, layer a hessian tablecloth with a stack of leather-bound books, silver candlesticks, a feathered bowl and a beaded ornamental necklace.

There is definitely an art to arranging and styling but with a little research and a keen eye for detail, anyone is capable of putting together a beautiful vignette. There are no hard and fast rules and you can't ever really go wrong with your groupings if they are meaningful to you.

Odd-number groupings are much more pleasing to the eye than even groupings. When in doubt, use the 'three, five or seven' rule, whereby items are always grouped together in odd numbers rather than even numbers. Grouping en masse is a great way to create visual impact.

Coloured groupings, when done well, add spark and life to a buffet table or entryway, and grouping 'like with like' is a sure way to create something special. Following the three-to-five colour rule by repeating colours through the vignette will serve you well, too.

If you feel you don't have a natural flair for putting lovely groupings together, follow the ingredients lists dotted throughout this book for a fail-safe formula.

Anchor piece: A statement artwork or a mirror.

Personality/character: An object with meaning behind it, such as an ornament collected on your overseas travels.

Odd-number groupings: Follow the 'three, five or seven' rule—the rule of three will work best for a small tabletop vignette.

Height: A table lamp or tall vase.

Layers: Stacked books or two picture frames of varying heights.

Styling

HOME

Flowers + styling

Use a coloured vase for extra impact. Clear vases show murky water much faster.

Flowers add so much to a room, from colour and scent to texture and visual weight. Flowers are like the lipstick of interiors and are an inexpensive way to add a luxe touch to any room. No space is complete without some living colour.

To get the most from your flowers, diagonally trim the soggy ends of the stem and change the water every two days.

POPULAR FLOWERS USED FOR STYLING

Roses are a timeless classic and the epitome of romance. Roses represent love and lust.

Ranunculus come in a variety of colours and their sweet, happy faces instantly brighten up a coffee table.

Poppies are cheerful, colourful and lively flowers, and playful room refreshers.

Hydrangeas are a classic staple in any grandmother's garden.

Tulips are a springtime favourite that come in a variety of colours.

Peonies are the ultimate wedding bouquet hero flower—they are soft, feminine and pretty, and come in colours from creamy whites to vibrant magentas.

Billy buttons are sunny yellow pompom flowers that make a bold statement grouped together on their own in a gorgeous bouquet. They last a long time once dried out, so you can keep them on display for months at a time.

Green ball dianthus are fluffy green balls, reminiscent of a drawing from a Dr. Seuss storybook. They are a relative of the carnation and add a quirky touch to a living room.

Kangaroo paw is an Australian native that comes in a variety of colours. It adds a beautiful touch of Australia to a room.

Protea, in particular the King Protea, is an architectural statement flower that is hardy and long lasting.

DECORATOR'S TIP

To arrange flowers neatly in a wide vase, use sticky tape to make a crisscross grid over the top of the vase, then poke the flower stems into the holes. This works well for flowers with short stems, as it prevents them from falling out of the vase.

Styling

HOME

Personalising your styling

Try not to get bogged down by the specifics of styling—it's meant to be a fun exercise, not a stressful activity. If you're finding it overwhelming, stop, leave the room and do something else. Having some time out can give you clarity and the willpower to finish styling when you enter the room again.

Use travel mementos, treasures you've inherited, gifts you've been given or items you've bought on a special occasion to tell a story in your vignette. These pieces all have special meaning to you and your family so they'll create interest when guests visit and instantly spark conversation.

It's easy to get caught up in buying as many 'things' as possible when redecorating, purely to fill a bookcase or mantel. However, if you take your time and collect items gradually, you'll end up much happier with the overall look because you will be surrounded by pieces that are meaningful to you.

Popular styling ingredients

Here's a go-to guide for the next time you're thinking of styling an area in your home and need some inspiration for what works well in a vignette.

- Books
- Vases
- Flowers
- Candles
- Ornaments
- Photo frames
- Candlesticks
- Clocks
- Dishes
- Catch-all dishes
- Bowls
- Jewellery trays
- Storage boxes
- Ceramic coasters
- Trays
- Shells
- Coral
- Air plants

Applying the elements of styling to your coffee table

INGREDIENTS

Tray
Vase
Flowers
Trinkets
Candle

TEXTURE

Your coffee table or tray will provide texture for the vignette, as will any soft materials you add.

CONTRAST

Use an array of objects on the coffee table to create visual interest.

METALLICS

Trinkets and knick-knacks are the perfect way to add a metallic touch to your coffee table vignette.

LIFE

No coffee table vignette is complete without a vase of flowers or small pot plant adding colour and love to the table.

PLACEMENT

Dividing the coffee table or tray into four sections will help you work out the object placement (see the Decorator's tip at right).

DECORATOR'S TIP

A tray will help keep your coffee table organised. Divide the tray into four sections to help you figure out where to place your items.

Section 1: *A tall object, such as a vase of flowers.*

Section 2: *A rounded object, such as a crystal-ball paperweight.*

Section 3: *An odd grouping, such as a stack of books.*

Section 4: *Something quirky, such as a treasured brass horse ornament.*

Styling

HOME

Applying the elements of styling to your mantel

TEXTURE

Textured wax pillar candles in grand candlestick holders placed either side of your artwork are a great addition to your mantel.

CONTRAST

Achieving balance on a long and narrow area can be difficult. For contrast, think tall candlesticks, cylindrical or spherical vases and quirky ornaments.

METALLICS

Try framing your art in a silver or gold frame and hanging it above the mantel for an elegant metallic touch.

LIFE

If the fireplace is in a room you use often, a fresh posy of flowers is a lovely way to inject some life into the space.

PLACEMENT

There are typically three options for ornament placement on the mantel. See the mantel styling options on the right to determine which will best suit your mantel.

Tall vase
Candlesticks
Picture frames
Flowers
Mirror
Art
Boxes
Trinkets

MANTEL STYLING OPTIONS

Centred: The easiest option when styling a mantel is to group your decorative pieces in the centre of the mantelpiece.

Symmetrical: Group the same types of items on either end of the mantel. For example, place two candlesticks on either side of a piece of art.

Anchor point: Group your decorative pieces with one stand-out anchor point that instantly draws the eye, along with other objects that are smaller. The anchor point doesn't have to be centred; it could be off-centre and have just as much impact.

Applying the elements of styling to your bookshelf

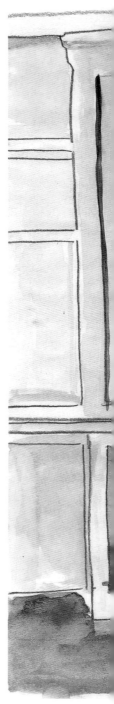

TEXTURE

Book spines provide the ultimate in texture for your bookshelf. Grouping them together with complementary materials is the easiest way to incorporate some texture.

CONTRAST

Add meaningful travel mementos in varying shapes and sizes to achieve a cohesive look on your bookshelf.

METALLICS

Add metallic ornaments where there are gaps between larger pieces. These little metallic elements will sparkle from the shelves.

LIFE

If the shelves aren't tall enough for a small posy of flowers to sit on, try placing a large indoor potted plant on the floor next to the bookshelf for that all-important touch of life and colour.

PLACEMENT

Group similar hues for a colour splash and bold statement on your shelves. Place your books on the shelves first, alternating horizontal with vertical stacking. Layer like objects together for more impact. For example, stacking a number of books horizontally on your shelf has much more weight and impact than one book on its own.

*Try leaning framed art
against the shelf as a nice
alternative to hanging art
and to fill a large gap on
your bookshelf.*

Styling

HOME

10

Decorator's guidebook

Rugs 101

DECORATOR'S TIP

Rubber backing or underlay will help prevent people from skidding on or tripping over your rug, especially on tiles and hardwood floors.

Rugs are considered the artwork of your floors. They also aid in anchoring and zoning off certain areas of a room by providing a visual perimeter for the furniture.

Where possible, it's best to have the front feet of large furniture on the edges of a rug rather than having the furniture sit around a smaller rug, making it look like a postage stamp. To help you visualise and decide on the right size rug for your room, lay some newspaper on the floor in the same shape and size as the rug you're considering.

COMMON MATERIALS

Sisal, hemp, sea grass or jute: These materials evoke a beachy, coastal, Hamptons vibe. They are brilliant for high-traffic areas, as they are hard-wearing and won't show sandy footprints easily. Shake them out regularly to keep them in good condition.

Wool: There are various ways a wool rug can be made—tufted, flat weave, knotted or woven—but each option is hard-wearing because wool is a natural fibre.

Wool and silk: One of the most luxurious rug compositions on the market, a blend of high-quality wool and silk results in a soft feeling underfoot and exudes class and elegance.

Digital prints: Digital images are printed onto low-pile acrylic or natural materials, allowing all manner of designs and patterns to appear on your floor.

Artificial and man-made fibres: These polypropylene materials are great for people with allergies as they are low-shed. Because they are machine-made, they are extremely durable. They are also a much more cost-effective option than wool.

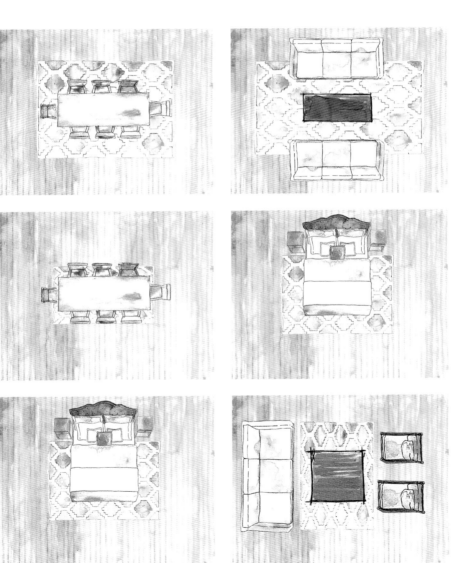

Decorator's guidebook

HOME

*A patterned rug with a solid
single-colour background will
hide stains and footprints well.*

- **Flatweave:** A thin, woven rug, typically wool or cotton.
- **Dhurrie:** Heavier than a flatweave and of Indian origin.
- **Kilim:** A thin, tapestry-woven rug.
- **Shag rug:** A deep-pile rug with a shaggy appearance.
- **Outdoor rug:** A durable rug, typically constructed from man-made materials such as acrylic or polypropylene, also often made from recycled plastic bottles.
- **Cow hide:** A durable rug, usually a by-product of the meat industry and ethically sourced.
- **Handmade rug:** A unique and one-of-a-kind rug.
- **Cotton:** A strong, soft rug, generally flat-woven; good for those with allergies, as it is a natural product.
- **Wool:** A warm, sturdy rug great for high-traffic areas.
- **Natural fibre:** A non-allergenic and earth-friendly option such as sisal, jute or hemp.
- **Synthetic:** Can mimic natural fibres but is generally not as long-lasting.

COMMON RUG PILES

- **Cut pile:** An upright pile with a luxurious look.
- **Loop pile:** An easy-care option that doesn't show footprints.
- **Cut and loop pile:** This combination creates a distinctive pattern and a rug that retains its crispness.
- **Multi-level loop pile:** Uses loops of various heights to create a textured finish.
- **Shag pile:** A long, rough pile.

Decorator's guidebook

HOME

Rectangular rugs are great for living rooms and bedrooms to anchor furniture or create different zones in the room.

Round rugs create interest in an entryway or open living area. They also broaden the horizontal illusion in a long, narrow space such as a hallway.

Square and oval rugs are less common but can be great under square dining tables or used as fillers for dead space.

DECORATOR'S TIP

Layering two rugs in very different materials adds to the cosy feeling of a room. Sisal as the base with a cow hide or Persian rug on top adds a degree of luxury to a living room or bedroom. Just make sure the rug on the bottom is much larger than the top rug so the room is framed properly.

Decorator's guidebook

HOME

Windows 101

Hang your curtains at ceiling height to make the room feel airy and the ceilings appear higher.

Window dressings play different roles in each room of the house. Some are purely decorative, some aid with filtering or blocking out light and others assist with privacy screening. Rooms never quite look finished until the windows are dressed appropriately. Choosing the right window coverings is important, as they tend to be expensive elements of the home that you don't replace very often.

TYPES OF WINDOW TREATMENTS

Full-length curtains: The curtain material neatly skims the floor but doesn't pool at the bottom. These curtains elongate the walls and make the room feel larger.

Half-length curtains: These curtains stop just under the edge of the windowsill or halfway down the wall. They can make the room feel smaller and can make the wall look unfinished if they stop too soon.

Roller blinds: Usually crafted from a sturdy, canvas-like material, roller blinds are great in bedrooms as they sit neatly within the window cavity and aid with blocking out light.

Roman blinds: Made from materials such as cotton or linen, Roman blinds are drawn up into a pleated gathering.

Venetian blinds: These horizontal, slatted timber blinds can be tilted up and down to control light and privacy.

Plantation shutters: These elegant, louvre-style shutters are made using horizontal timber slats and are typically fixed to the window or hinged so they open as one panel. They are costly, but a worthwhile investment.

CURTAIN MATERIALS

Sheers: These are made using lighter fabrics, often cotton, and are usually white.

Block-out: A great choice for those who can't sleep in a room that's not completely dark. They allow almost no light to get in and are excellent for privacy screening.

Linen: Gritty linens add an elegant yet relaxed feel.

Cotton: Cotton is the most common curtain material. It allows flexibility with colour and pattern.

Silk: This is the choice for a stately manor that requires bold, grand curtains. Rich jewel tones work best for silk curtains.

Velvet: This is a much heavier material that exudes a luxurious, almost regal feel.

CURTAIN DETAILS

- **Pelmet:** A narrow border that conceals the curtain fittings.
- **Tie-back:** A strip of fabric or cord that holds the curtains open.
- **Rods and finials:** The rods hold the curtains up, while the finials can be fitted to their ends.
- **Curtain heading:** The top of the curtain. Options include box pleats, tie, pencil pleats, pinch pleats.

Layering your window treatments will give you more control over light filtering and privacy screening, which is especially important for bedrooms with street frontage. For example, a beautiful way to filter light and provide privacy in the evening is to combine Roman blinds inset into a window cavity with soft, sheer, floor-length curtains hung over the top of the window frame.

Decorator's guidebook

HOME

Cushions 101

Scatter cushions are one of the most effective styling elements in a home. A sofa looks naked without some cushions, and your bed will be a boring collection of linen without a few cushions arranged on top.

Cushions can be a controversial element, as many people deem them unnecessary fluff. However, when they are selected carefully, cushions have the power to transform your room, tie together your colour palette and also provide a comfortable and cosy spot for you to snuggle into on the sofa.

TYPES OF CUSHIONS

- Square
- Lumbar
- Box square
- Round
- Box round
- Bolster

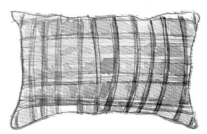

Candles 101

Candles are an important styling element for your home. They diffuse a beautiful scent and the jars that hold them can add interest in the form of colour, texture and pattern. Where possible, opt for candles made from more natural ingredients, such as beeswax, coconut wax, soy wax or a natural soy blend, to avoid nasty toxins burning in your home.

Candles come in so many different shapes and sizes that you should be able to find some that suit your home's decor. A collection of candles grouped together on a coffee table can have just as much visual impact as a bunch of flowers. Once your candles have burnt all the way through you can re-use the jar or canister as a vase.

GETTING THE MOST FROM YOUR CANDLES

When lighting a candle for the first time, allow the wax to melt all the way to the edge to ensure a clean burn for the life of the candle. This may take a couple of hours, so make sure you will be spending enough time in the room before you light it so that you can keep an eye on it.

Before you relight the candle, trim the wick, snipping off the untidy ends to stop black smoky marks forming on the inside of the candle jar or canister. If you don't trim the wick, you will accelerate the burn time, making the candle burn out much faster.

Avoid burning your candle near an open window or air vent, as this will also speed up the burn time significantly.

Lighting 101

Lighting is one of the most important elements in decorating. Lights add texture, colour and pattern to a room and can often be a talking point.

TYPES OF LIGHTING

- Floor lamps
- Table lamps
- Pendants
- Wall sconces
- Chandeliers
- Candles

LAMPSHADE OPTIONS

- Drum
- Tapered
- Square
- Spherical

LAMPSHADE TRIM OPTIONS

- Pompoms
- Ribbon
- Fringe

PURPOSES OF LIGHTING

Task lighting: Lighting can aid in specific tasks, such as reading or painting.

Ambience and mood: Lighting is an all-important element for enhancing the atmosphere and feel of a room.

Additional lighting: If your room doesn't receive enough natural light, additional overhead lighting can mimic sunlight.

Focal point lighting: Lighting can enhance or draw attention to a beautiful piece of artwork or other decorative item.

DECORATOR'S TIP

Two table lamps placed at either end of a console table or buffet create symmetry and balance while also providing a great source of light for the room.

Decorator's guidebook

HOME

Art 101

Average eye level is 150 cm (5 ft) from the ground, so hang your art centred to that height on the wall.

Have you ever entered a home that didn't have any artwork hanging on the walls? A room feels bare and barren without artwork. Art has the power to transform and breathe life into a room, while also tying the colour palette together.

You don't have to visit galleries and buy large expensive pieces to fill your walls; there are so many affordable art options on the market that it's not necessary to break the bank.

Use your imagination when placing the art in your home. There are many alternatives, from gallery-style feature walls to a solo statement piece filling an entire wall. Often framing a single striking piece of art in a beautiful frame is all that is required to transform it into a statement piece. If you want to make a feature from a number of prints, cluster framing is likely your best option.

Cluster framing is a popular way to display family photos, with focal lighting shining down from the wall to really draw attention to the display. Hanging a collection of nine or more prints in similar frames will give your walls the 'wow' factor.

Leaning your art against a wall on top of a big furniture piece rather than mounting it on the wall is also a great way to add a pop of colour to a room. This is a great option for renters who don't want to make holes in the walls.

GALLERY LAYOUTS

- Square
- Rectangular
- Vertical
- Horizontal

DECORATOR'S TIP

*When hanging art above
a sofa, leave approximately
30 cm (12 in) from
the top of the sofa to the
bottom of the art to allow
for heads to rest back on
the wall without knocking
the artwork.*

11

Resource book

Online resources

A Beautiful Mess www.abeautifulmess.com

Apartment Therapy www.apartmenttherapy.com

Bright.Bazaar www.brightbazaarblog.com

Cococozy www.cococozy.com

Cupcakes and Cashmere www.cupcakesandcashmere.com

Decor8 www.decor8blog.com

Design Sponge www.designsponge.com

Eat Read Love www.eatreadlove.com

Interiors Addict www.theinteriorsaddict.com

Ish & Chi www.ishandchi.com

Kate Waterhouse www.katewaterhouse.com

Lauren Liess www.laurenliess.com

Rebecca Judd Loves www.rebeccajuddloves.com

The Design Files www.thedesignfiles.net

The Joye www.thejoye.com

Yellowtrace www.yellowtrace.com.au

Brit + Co www.brit.co

Captain & The Gypsy Kid www.captainandthegypsykid.com

Glitter Guide www.theglitterguide.com

Goop www.goop.com

HomeStyleFile www.homestylefile.com.au

Houzz www.houzz.com.au

Milray Park www.milraypark.com

Minutes Matter www.minutesmatter.com

Mydoma Studio www.mydomastudio.com

Olioboard www.olioboard.com

Pinterest www.pinterest.com

Refinery 29 www.refinery29.com

Show and Tell Online www.showandtellonline.com.au

Table Tonic www.tabletonic.com.au

The Everygirl www.theeverygirl.com

The Grace Tales www.thegracetales.com

Resource book

HOME

Adore Home Magazine
www.adoremagazine.com

Est www.estliving.com

Heart Home www.hearthomemag.co.uk

Lonny www.lonny.com

Matchbook www.matchbookmag.com

Rue www.ruemag.com

The Home Magazine www.thehome.com.au

Winkelen www.issuu.com/winkelen

Apps

TOOLS

Converter

Spirit Level

FLOOR PLANS AND ROOM PLANNERS

Houseplan

Magicplan

Room Planner

MOOD BOARDS

Mood Board

Morpholio Board

Software

Google SketchUp

Icovia Online Interior Design Software

RoomSketcher

Resource book

HOME

Index

Index

HOME

Acknowledgements

Working on this book has taught me valuable lessons in balance, time management, organisation and efficiency. Most importantly, it has reinforced to me that I do actually know what I'm talking about.

Being a solo business owner means that I draw on support from a huge range of people and businesses to get projects off the ground. This book wouldn't have come together without the help and support of a number of very special people.

Firstly, I am very grateful to the team at Hardie Grant, in particular Loran McDougall, Justine Harding and Jane Willson. Thank you, Jane, for your enthusiasm about my book concept and for helping me bring it to life. I'm thrilled to be able to add the title of 'author' to my résumé.

Maddison Rogers, my wonderfully talented and dedicated illustrator, I have no doubt that you have a very long, successful and fulfilling career ahead of you. I can't thank you enough for translating my vision for the book into this beautiful work of art.

Thank you to the numerous retailers who have hosted my decorating workshops in their stores. Your excitement for homewares and decorating keeps driving me further.

Over the years I have collected a wonderful group of friends from the design industry. They inspire me daily to push the decorating boundaries and so many of the lessons I have learned with them have made their way into this book. Particular thanks must go to Sonya Pala for her never-ending passion and support, and to Elyse Daniels for being my sounding-board and business buddy. Thank you also to my colleagues at thehome.com.au. I thoroughly enjoy working with such a talented bunch.

Mum and Dad, thank you for always telling me I am capable of succeeding in anything I do and for encouraging my independent, entrepreneurial spirit. You have inspired me to work hard, to never give up without a fight and to be happy in life. To my brothers, Alexander and Luke … you desperately need to read this book. And thank you to my grandmothers, Shirley and Markie, for clipping every magazine article I'm quoted in and sticking it on the fridge. This one might be too big for the fridge!

Last, but not least, thank you to my lovely clients, past and present, and followers in the social media world. Many of you have become real-life friends and I am so grateful to you all for your encouragement and interest in what I do.

About the author

Emma isn't one to sit still. She runs a successful interior styling business (emmablomfield.com) and in 2015 she launched The Decorating School, an online school that teaches homeowners how to decorate their homes with confidence. These roles make use of her natural flair for interiors and styling, her passion for online marketing and ecommerce and her unrivalled knowledge of homewares and furniture suppliers.

Emma's previous experience as a property stylist and with an online furniture and homewares store gave her the industry exposure she needed to set up her own business. She spotted a gap in the market for e-decorating and has pioneered making interior design accessible, affordable and available via the web to homeowners and renters across Australia.

Emma consults in person in Sydney. Her high-profile jobs include styling the homes of pop star Guy Sebastian and *X-Factor* winner Samantha Jade. She also travels around Australia, bringing her decorating knowledge to a wider audience by teaming up with homewares retailers and teaching locals the principles of decorating and styling through interactive workshops.

A keen networker, Emma attends many industry events and has her finger firmly on the pulse. She has a strong social media following and has appeared in numerous TV segments, magazines and newspapers, demonstrating her styling skills.

HOME

Published in 2017 by Hardie Grant Books,
an imprint of Hardie Grant Publishing

Hardie Grant Books (Melbourne)
Building 1, 658 Church Street
Richmond, Victoria 3121
hardiegrantbooks.com.au

Hardie Grant Books (London)
5th & 6th Floors
52–54 Southwark Street
London SE1 1UN
hardiegrantbooks.co.uk

A Cataloguing-in-Publication entry is available from the catalogue of
the National Library of Australia at www.nla.gov.au

Home: The Elements of Decorating
ISBN 978 1 74379 271 1

Publishing Director: Jane Willson
Managing Editor: Marg Bowman
Project Editor: Loran McDougall
Editor: Justine Harding
Design Managers: Vaughan Mossop and Mark Campbell
Designer: Murray Batten
Illustrator: Maddison Rogers
Typesetter: Patrick Cannon
Production Manager: Todd Rechner
Production Coordinator: Rebecca Bryson

Colour reproduction by Splitting Image Colour Studio
Printed in China by 1010 Printing International Limited